Linn's

Guide to
Stamp Collecting
Software
and Collecting on the Internet

William F. Sharpe

Published by *Linn's Stamp News*, the largest and most informative stamp newspaper in the world. *Linn's* is owned by Amos Press Inc., 911 Vandemark Road, Sidney, Ohio 45365. Amos Press also publishes *Scott Stamp Monthly* and the Scott line of catalogs. This book and its cover were designed by Veronica Schreiber.

Contents

Introduction

The headline over my first article in *Linn's Stamp News* in 1983 read "Don't Buy Computer Just for Stamp Collection." I suggested then that a computer was a great tool for a collector, but the cost of a computer wasn't justified if that's the only reason a person wanted a computer. Several readers disagreed with me then and pointed out that the only reason they had purchased a computer was to use it in connection with their stamp hobby.

Considering all the advances made in the past 13 years in the realm of personal computers, I would rephrase my recommendation. Go out and buy a computer for your hobby, even if that's the only reason you want to buy one. You'll soon find many other uses for a computer.

There are three kinds of people in the world — those who make things happen, those who watch things happen and those who wonder what happened. I'd expect most readers to be in the first group, a few might be in the second group and none in the third.

This book concentrates on stamp-related computer usage. There are two primary areas where collectors use computers: stamp inventory and album/exhibit-page preparation. I'll get to other areas, such as the Internet, but these two are by far the main ones.

A survey conducted by *Linn's* in 1996 showed that 34 percent of its readers use a computer in connection with their hobby. This is supported by a recent American Philatelic Society poll that revealed that an almost identical percentage used the machines in some fashion related to their hobby.

I'll look at both hardware and software. Don't look here for brand-name recommendations on which hardware manufacturers are best. There are many computer magazines available with advice on what to buy and what to avoid.

The stamp-related programs mentioned here were available at the time this book was written. The computer world is fast-moving; companies come and go. I provide names, addresses and phone numbers, where known. I urge you to contact vendors prior to placing orders to make sure programs are still available and that the price hasn't changed. I have tried to be comprehensive, but I'm sure there are excellent programs that I'm just not aware of. Several organizations did not respond to my requests for information. If I did not hear from them, I did not include them in my listing of programs.

Information provided about the Internet is even more ephemeral than programs. Web sites come and go, addresses change. If you can't locate a site by the URL (Uniform Resource Locator) address I provide, try using a search engine to find its current location. Most Internet providers and online services furnish one or more search engines for this purpose.

I'm sure there will be a few disappointed Macintosh users reading this book. There are very few dedicated stamp programs for these people. I located three inventory programs and no album-page programs. One inventory program is a template (outline) for a commercial program; one is a program that comes in Mac, DOS and Windows versions; and the third is a program the author never forwarded to me. Mac users can, of course, access all the information and stamp images available on the Internet.

Primer
Some Basics about Computers

This is a brief introduction to computers in general. Feel free to skip to Chapter 1 if you're already familiar with computers.

A computer system consists of four parts: input, processing, output and storage. Basically, any computer system accepts data input, processes it, delivers the output as information in some fashion and provides storage for programs, data and information.

You can compare a computer to a simple stereo system made up of a compact disk (CD) player, an amplifier and a pair of speakers. The CD player converts the physical patterns on the tracks into sounds and sends them to the amplifier as electronic signals. The amplifier strengthens the signals and sends them on to the speakers. The result is music. The CD player is an input device, the amplifier is a processing unit, and the speakers are output devices. The CD itself is a storage device.

A more complex stereo system might include a tape recorder and a radio. You can either play music from a tape or record music to a tape. The tape can be considered as an example of input/output media. Hard disks and floppy disks are also considered input/output media, since you can get data into your computer from these disks as well as place information on the disk from the computer.

Data are essentially raw facts. Virtually any kind of facts can become computer data: a letter, a budget, a list of stamps. Computers handle four types of data: text, graphics, audio and video. Most of the time we don't want to get data back from the computer in the same form that we entered them. We want the computer to process the data and give us useful information. We might want a list of our stamps sorted with the most valuable stamps first. Or we may want to see only those stamps issued before 1900. A topical collector of railroad stamps may want to list only those stamps that show steam engines.

Besides data, computers also need programs to operate. Programs are instructions that tell the computer how to process data to produce the results that you want.

Personal computers are general-purpose devices. They can perform a variety of tasks; they depend on program instructions for guidance. The program and its inputs direct the circuits in the computer to open and close in the manner needed to perform a specific task. Each computer circuit is a switch, which is either on or off. Eight of these on-off switches make up a byte, which is considered the basic unit for memory storage. Consider a byte as storing one character of information, such as the letter "a." A kilobyte (kb) is 1,024 bytes, a megabyte (Mb) is about 1 million bytes, and a gigabyte (GB) is about 1 billion bytes.

There are two types of storage associated with computers: primary and secondary. Primary storage holds the data and programs that the computer is currently processing. The 16 megabytes of memory that you see listed in computer advertisements is primary storage. This memory is fast but volatile. Volatile means that the contents of memory disappear when the computer is turned off. Secondary storage is located on peripheral devices, such as a hard or floppy disk or a CD-ROM. This storage is considered permanent, although you can delete or modify data from disks as desired.

Hard disks have the capability to store several gigabytes of data. A typical floppy disk can store 1.44 megabytes. A CD-ROM holds up to 650 megabytes. The ROM designation stands for Read-Only Memory, which means that you can get data from a CD-ROM but you can't write information to it. Manufacturers are now selling CD-ROM recorders at affordable prices (under $700), which allow writing to a blank CD-ROM disk, but only one time. A stamp image saved at 100 dots-per-inch resolution would typically require 25 kilobytes of storage. You could store 26,000 such images on one CD-ROM.

The main input device for a personal computer is the keyboard. Other input devices include the mouse, scanner, microphone, bar-code reader, joystick, light pen and trackball. The chief output device is a monitor. Other output devices are printers, plotters and speakers.

The benefits that personal computers provide can be summarized as helping individuals work more efficiently or more effectively. Efficiency relates to how well a job is done. Computers can do certain kinds of work faster than humans and with fewer errors. If you decide that the value of your stamp collection has increased because of inflation, you could increase the value of each stamp by 3 percent. Assuming that you're using a program equipped with the proper commands, the computer can update each stamp's value very quickly. Effectiveness relates to doing the right thing. As an example, a computer can create products that would otherwise be impossible, an example being special movie effects.

Chapter 1

Hardware

Hardware is the computer stuff you can see and trip over.

You may already own a computer, or you may be thinking of upgrading your equipment. You may just be thinking about buying a computer.

Much of the software I'll be discussing, particularly for album-page preparation, requires a graphical interface to run and won't work on older equipment. I still get an occasional letter from an Apple II, Radio Shack TRS or Commodore 64 user, complaining that there aren't any stamp programs available for their equipment or that I never mention their machines in my column. If you are using one of these computers, you won't find anything in this book applicable to these machines. You may want to read on with the thought of upgrading your equipment so you can take advantage of more recent programs.

If you're thinking about purchasing a new computer, you have essentially two choices — an IBM-compatible machine or an Apple Macintosh. The Macintosh, introduced in 1984, is an excellent machine, easy to learn to use. But the Mac comprises less than 10 percent of the market. Almost all the remaining machines use a Microsoft operating system, either text-based MS-DOS or a graphical system, Windows, Windows for Workgroups, Windows 95 or Windows NT.

Compared to the Windows/DOS machines, there aren't that many programs around for the Macintosh, particularly when you get into specialized areas like stamp collecting. I have not located an album-page preparation program for the Mac. That's a shame, because the Mac has excellent graphic capabilities.

Does that mean you shouldn't buy a Macintosh if you are a collector who wants to design album pages? Not at all. You just won't be able to use a program that's set up specifically for stamp collectors. You can create fine album pages with word processors, spreadsheets and especially desktop-publishing programs. And there are a number of such programs for the Mac. One Macintosh user states that he feels fortunate in not having to go through all the contortions that DOS and Windows users do. He maintains his inventories using FileMakerPro, designs his album and information pages in QuarkXpress, and manipulates his scanned images in Adobe Photoshop.

Given the pace of computer technology, you have to accept the fact that the computer you buy today will be obsolete tomorrow (and I mean the day after today, not a metaphorical date in the future). Several people who don't own a computer have told me they are waiting for new microprocessor chips, bigger hard disks, cheaper memory and overall reduced prices before they buy a new machine. So they wait. And when they do buy a computer, prices continue to decline, new chips appear and their equipment becomes obsolete anyway. I'm not saying you should replace your computer just because it's two years old; if you are happy with your current machine, continue using it. But if you're contemplating a computer purchase, now is the time to buy.

I said I wouldn't mention brand names for computer purchase. I will suggest, though, that you buy a Pentium or equivalent machine with 16 megabytes of memory, a 15-inch color monitor, a mouse, a CD-ROM drive, Windows 95 and as large a hard disk as you can afford. Consider a portable computer only if you need to take the machine to stamp shows. The price differential is decreasing, but you'll still pay considerably more for the same power in a portable machine than for a desktop.

You'll also need a printer. Laserjets give excellent printouts but are pricey. You can get almost as good results with an inkjet printer at a much lower cost. You don't really need color, but there's not much of a price penalty to buy a color inkjet printer and the resulting printouts are impressive. The cheapest color inkjets provide one cartridge with three primary-color compartments; a black printout is a combination of the three colors and doesn't look nearly as good as a regular monochrome printed page. Get a machine that includes an additional black cartridge for those pages that don't require color. Your printer cost will soar if you insist on printing album pages much larger than the standard 8½ by 11 inches. There are some workarounds that people have mentioned to get slightly larger pages, but the simple approach is to accept the fact that your album pages will be this size. Printer paper is much cheaper and more readily available in this standard size. Brother manufactures a laser printer, Model HL-420, that accepts paper and envelopes up to 9 by 12 inches. The printer features a straight-path paper feed and sells for under $400.

You'll want at least a 28.8 kbps modem if you plan to access the Internet or online services. Modems come in two flavors, internal and external. An internal modem card fits into an expansion slot in your computer case; you attach a phone cord between a plug on the back of the card and a phone jack. The external modem is a separate box that plugs into the serial port of your computer. You also need to attach the phone cord. Internal modems are cheaper and don't take up any desk space, but you must have an available expansion slot in your computer case.

You may want a scanner if you plan to place images or enlargements of your stamps on your album pages. A hand-held scanner is sufficient for most work with stamps, since stamps are small and the scanner can handle widths up to about 4½ inches. It's easy to scan stamps if you place them in a transparent acetate sleeve so they won't move when you pass the scanner over them. If you buy a color printer, get a color scanner, too. Hand-held scanners generally include software that allows you to "stitch" together two passes to obtain a complete page. My experience has been that the stitching process is problematic at best. Get a flat-plate scanner that will handle a full page with one pass if you expect to scan complete album pages or entire sheets rather than individual stamps. A flat-plate scanner will take up a lot of desk real estate.

Software

Software comprises the programs you run in your computer, including the operating system. Without software, your computer is one big door stop.

You have several choices in this area. You can buy programs that have been specifically designed for stamp collectors, use commercial programs that can be adapted to a stamp collector's needs or write your own programs using a programming language such as BASIC, C or Pascal.

The advantage of programs designed for collectors is that it's easy to use the program right after installation. Many of these programs include a built-in database of stamp information so you can avoid tedious entry of data for each of your stamps. Often, though, these programs are inflexible; you can't add specific topical information that's important to you or delete the information you don't care about.

Advantages of commercial programs, such as word processors, spreadsheets or database-management systems, include the flexibility of setting them up so that only the information you are interested in is required. If you already are using Microsoft Excel as a spreadsheet, there's no additional cost or learning curve involved in adapting the application for your collection.

You get maximum flexibility by writing your own program, if you are willing to take the time and trouble to learn a programming language. This approach, though, seems like reinventing the wheel for most people. The newer spreadsheet programs include formatting, searching and sorting capabilities with no programming required.

At one time, the recommended approach for a new computer purchase was to select the software you planned to use,

then buy the computer that was required to run that software. Personal computer specifications are so standardized today that, except in unusual circumstances, you can buy a machine and expect to run any software program on it.

The following summaries and charts provide information about a number of dedicated stamp-inventory programs, i.e., programs written specifically for stamp collectors. As I stated in the introduction, the information is current as this book is written, but prices change, new versions are offered, and suppliers move or go out of business. Call or write the company before you send a check to purchase anything. A company that doesn't respond to a sales inquiry won't likely respond to a later question asking how to use the program.

Inventory programs range from shareware programs selling for $10 to complete programs including stamp images on CD-ROMs for $100. In general, the less-expensive programs do not include a built-in database of stamp information. That means the user must enter details about each stamp by keyboard entry. Built-in databases provide extensive information about the stamp; generally, the user only needs to indicate the stamp is owned, the quantity owned and the stamp condition.

You can obtain current information, including program version numbers, from the Philatelic Computer Study Group website at: www.west.net/~stamps1/invintro.htm. (Note that there's a "one" following "stamps" in the above address.)

The list includes hypertext links so you can contact vendors with web pages for their products. E-mail links are also provided where known.

What the Rating Categories Mean

The number in parenthesis is the weighting factor for each of the categories. The total is 100. A program with a superb rating for documentation would receive the full 20 points; very fine, 16; fine, 12; etc. The overall value is the summation of all the individual categories.

You can construct your own rating system by assigning more points to one category and fewer to another. If you never read a manual, you might assign no points to documentation and 30 points to ease of use.

Documentation (20) — Is the manual easy to understand? Are figures and examples of operation included? Is there an index? Is there a table of contents? Are step-by-step instructions given for all operations? Does the manual include installation instructions?

Access speed (10) — Does the program start quickly? Are there any noticeable delays in switching from one screen display to another when running the program? If sorting and searching capabilities are included, do these operations proceed quickly?

Ease of use (10) — Does the program include mouse support? Are the menu choices intuitive? Is it easy to set up report formats? Is there an online help system provided with the program? A few of these inventory programs are quite powerful and therefore somewhat complex. Is it relatively easy to learn to use these programs? Can the more complex features be ignored, if desired? Are toolbars provided for mouse users? Are shortcut keys provided for typists?

Readability (10) — Are the screen displays cluttered with too much information? Are status-line displays included to provide more information about menu or toolbar choices?

Room for notes (5) — Can the user add comments to the information about his stamps? How much room is provided for these comments? Some collectors may want to write a paragraph or two about a particular stamp.

Allows duplication (5) — Can the user set up multiple entries for one catalog number to cover different conditions for various stamps: used, mint, blocks, condition, on cover, and so on.?

Customization (10) — Can the user add or delete fields? Some collectors only want to keep track of a catalog number and a price; others may want to include much additional information about their stamps.

Reporting (10) — Are reports included? If so, how many formats are available? Can the user customize reports? Can reports be displayed on screen or saved as a separate file as well as being printed?

Ease of installation (10) — Are printed instructions available? These can be as simple as a line or two of instructions on a floppy-disk label. Does the program install properly with no error messages displayed on screen? If auxiliary files are required in addition to the main program file, are these automatically installed? Can the program be uninstalled, i.e., removed, easily?

After-sales support (10) — Is there a phone number for contacting the program provider? An e-mail address? A web site? Are updates available? How frequently?

Collect!

This modest program allows you to set up a maximum of eight data fields. You define the name of the field and specify how it is to be used, either as text or numbers. You can also create a pick list, which should contain the major categorization for each field. Up to 10,000 records can be created for each data file. The program might be best suited for someone with a small topical collection.

You can attach a text file to any record with descriptive information ranging up to 30,000 characters. You can also specify a graphic file showing an image of your stamp. The program doesn't include any pre-entered data or stamp images.

Limited printing options are available, but they may be sufficient for your needs. You can send your report to a named file, then examine the results in a text editor before using up paper resources to see what your report looks like.

This program is part of a package called ASL Home that includes management of other collections, investments and recipes. It also includes a 256-color paint program.

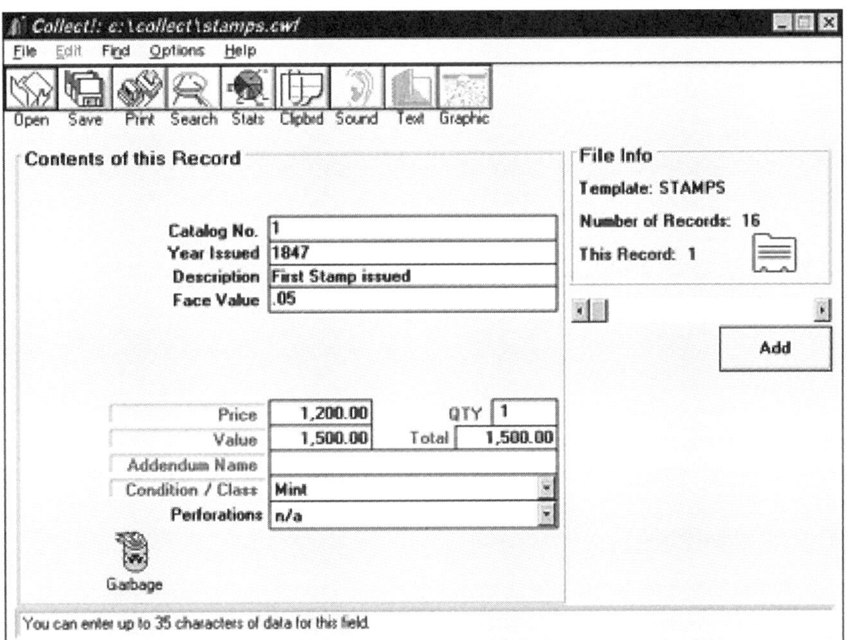

Collect!

Written for: Windows
Database included: no
Annual updates: no
Stamp images: user-specified images can
    be included in program
Price: $24.95
Address: Alston Labs
    P.O. Box 581
    Ruidoso NM 88345
Phone: (209) 522-8666
One-line summary: very flexible,
    user-defined database format

	superb (1.00)	very fine (0.80)	fine (0.60)	average (0.40)	poor (0)	value
documentation (20)				•		8
access speed (10)	•					10
ease of use (10)	•					10
readability (10)	•					10
room for notes (5)	•					5
allows duplication (5)	•					5
customization (10)	•					10
reporting (10)				•		4
ease of installation (10)	•					10
after-sale support (10)		•				8
overall value (100)						80

Collector's Assistant

This program runs in DOS and supports the use of a mouse, tab keys or Alt-plus-letter key navigation around the menus and entry screens. Mouse movement in an MS-DOS window under Windows 95 was very sluggish, but running the program in pure MS-DOS mode outside Windows 95 resolved this problem.

Documentation is limited to a four-page README.TXT file, which describes the operation of the program. A sample file would have been helpful. The data entry screen is not user-friendly. The program requires that you enter a value for the color of your stamp, whether or not you want to keep track of this stamp feature. I added NA (for not applicable) to the list of available colors. If I did not include the color, the program gave me an error message. When you save a file in the program, the DOS commands are echoed on your screen on top of the menu that appears there. No harm is done, but this seems disconcerting rather than useful.

You cannot modify the fields that come with the program. There's a note field on the entry screen, but it is limited to about six characters. You can create three types of reports. You can attach a stamp image to each stamp record, but you'll need to create or obtain the images elsewhere. Only GIF and PCX formats are supported.

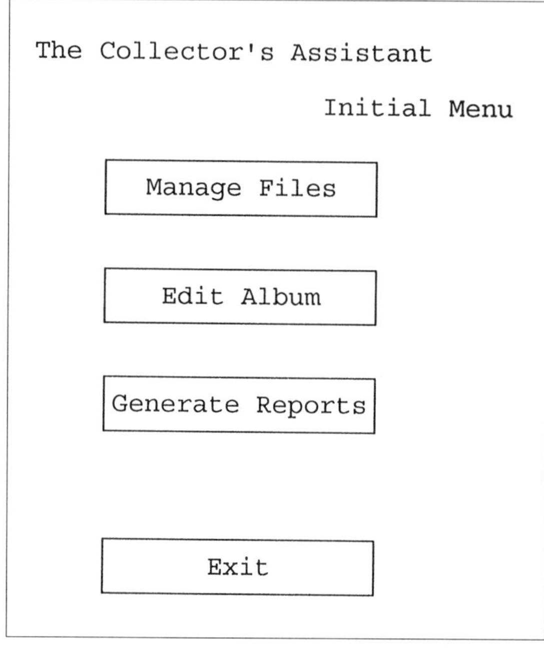

Collector's Assistant

Written for: DOS
Database included: no
Annual updates: no
Stamp images: can be added by user
Price: $18.50
Address: Edward May
    P.O. Box 71012
    Pittsburgh, PA 15213
Phone: (412) 731-0622
One-line summary: inflexible program; data entry is especially tedious

	superb (1.00)	very fine (0.80)	fine (0.60)	average (0.40)	poor (0)	value
documentation (20)				•		8
access speed (10)		•				8
ease of use (10)				•		4
readability (10)		•				8
room for notes (5)					no	0
allows duplication (5)	•					5
customization (10)					•	0
reporting (10)				•		4
ease of installation (10)	•					10
after-sale support (10)			•			6
overall value (100)						53

Estam

Three separate programs are well-integrated in this group: Stamp Valuer, Auction Valuer and Stamp Finder. Stamp Finder offers six menu choices to locate stamps: Scott number, year of issue, stamp denomination, stamp color, description and an ordered list.

Once you have obtained the Scott number of the stamp you're interested in, you can use the Valuer to obtain a retail price. For more valuable stamps, there are nine grades regarding margins and centering, ranging from superb to off-color. There are five gum grades plus a factor for stamp faults. If you don't choose otherwise, Valuer assumes that your stamp is fine to very fine for margins, is never hinged with original gum and has no faults. You can obtain valuation for a series of stamps, assuming all stamps are of the same condition. Valuer calculated that Scott numbers 1 through 1000 had a total value of $1,681,267.63. On the other hand, the numbers from 1001 through 2000 were only worth $452.75. You can use Valuer to create an inventory or want list for your stamps.

Estam supplies a short, well-written stamp-grading guide that explains how to assess the value of a stamp. Sample photographs illustrate each centering grade in detail. Data files for these programs are quite compact, taking up less than 1 megabyte of memory.

```
 ________________________________________________________________
|                                                                |
|   ┌───────────┤ T h e   E S T A M   S T A M P   V A L U E R ├──────┐   |
| P │                 ┌─────── M A I N   M E N U ───────┐         │ P |
| R │                 │                                 │         │ R |
| O │                                                             │ O |
| G │        1    Value Stamps, Sets or Runs                      │ G |
| R │                                                             │ R |
| A │        2    Value a Lot or Collection                       │ A |
| M │                                                             │ M |
|   │        3    Inventory: Enter, Display, Update               │   |
| O │                                                             │ O |
| P │        4    Want Lists: Enter, Display, Revise              │ P |
| T │                                                             │ T |
| I │        5    Note Pad                                        │ I |
| O │                                                             │ O |
| N │        6    Stamp Finder Program                            │ N |
| S │                                                             │ S |
|   │                 Enter Number or use Highlight Bars ─┘         │   |
| ║                                                                │   |
| ╚═ For Collections of William F. Sharpe ═══════════════════════════   |
|                                                                |
|    F1 Help                                   F10 Terminate Program   |
|________________________________________________________________|
```

Estam

Written for: DOS
Database included: yes
Annual updates: no
Stamp images: no
Price: $39.95
Address: Forrest H. Blanding
     6 Cornell Road
     Cranford, NJ 07016
Phone: (908) 276-5132
One-line summary: very fast search results
    and well-written grading guide

	superb (1.00)	very fine (0.80)	fine (0.60)	average (0.40)	poor (0)	value
documentation (20)	•					20
access speed (10)	•					10
ease of use (10)	•					10
readability (10)		•				8
room for notes (5)					no	0
allows duplication (5)					no	0
customization (10)				•		4
reporting (10)				•		4
ease of installation (10)	•					10
after-sale support (10)		•				8
overall value (100)						74

EZ Stamp

EZ Stamp combines a basic stamp-inventory system with color images for all stamps provided in the database. You can also add more stamps, either for a new country or to an existing database. Stamp images are stored on the CD-ROM, not on your hard disk, and are accessible outside the EZ Stamp program.

The data-entry screen is divided into two parts: condition and detail, where the user enters information about each stamp, and Scott's related information, which cannot be modified. You can search through the database file using either the year of issue or Minkus number. A variety of report formats are available, which can be displayed on the screen or sent to your printer.

You can order the program for $79.99 and receive images and databases for a total of 37 countries, including the United States, Canada, United Nations, Germany, Great Britian, Ireland and Cyprus.

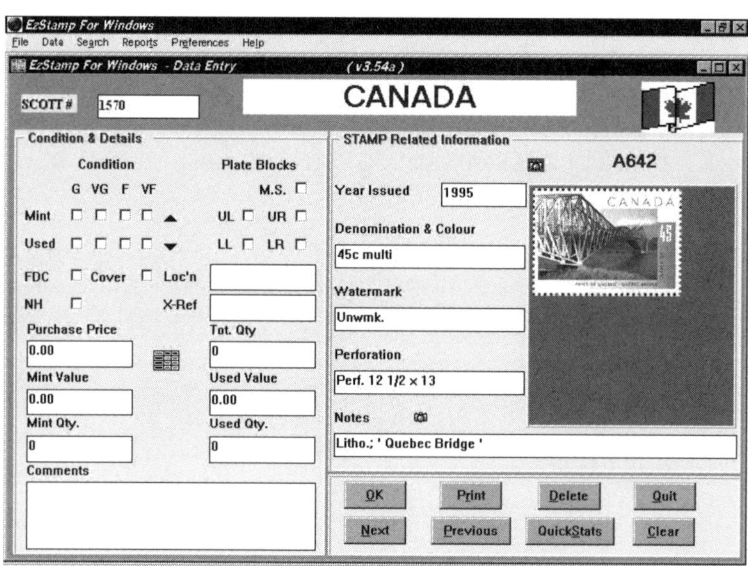

EZ Stamp

Written for: Windows
Database included: yes
Annual updates: yes
Stamp images: yes
Price: $79.99 plus $5 shipping
Address: Softpro 2001
    18 Levberhume Crescent
    Scarborough, Ontario, Canada M1E 1K4
Phone: (416) 261-7763
E-mail: marios@msn.com
Internet: www.subwaystamp.com/ez-mega.htm
One-line summary: excellent integration of
    database and CD-ROM stamp images

	superb (1.00)	very fine (0.80)	fine (0.60)	average (0.40)	poor (0)	value
documentation (20)		•				16
access speed (10)	•					10
ease of use (10)	•					10
readability (10)		•				8
room for notes (5)		•				4
allows duplication (5)	•					5
customization (10)			•			6
reporting (10)			•			6
ease of installation (10)	•					10
after-sale support (10)	•					10
overall value (100)						85

HobbySoft

Originally titled CompuQuote, the HobbySoft Stamp Keeper programs have been available since 1986. Versions for DOS, Windows and Macintosh are now marketed by Ninga Software Corporation in Canada. You get one database with your purchase; additional databases are $20 each. Databases include U.S. singles, U.S. plate blocks, Canada, United Nations, Germany, East Germany, Great Britain and Israel.

Each database consists of Scott numbers, descriptions and market values. Stamps not listed in the database can be added by the user. You can create group entries to enter ownership information about a series of stamps, provided the information (quantity, condition) is identical for all stamps.

Stamp Keeper provides standard reports plus the capability to generate custom reports. You can specify which fields of your stamp record are printed, in what order, and conditions about which entries to include. For example, you could create a report listing only those stamps issued prior to 1940 that are worth $100 or more. Stamp Keeper has the most flexible report-generating capabilities of any inventory program in this group.

You can also display an on-screen calculator or a calendar/diary program with a text field allowing entries for any day of the year. The manual is concise at 32 pages, but it provides all the necessary information for running the program.

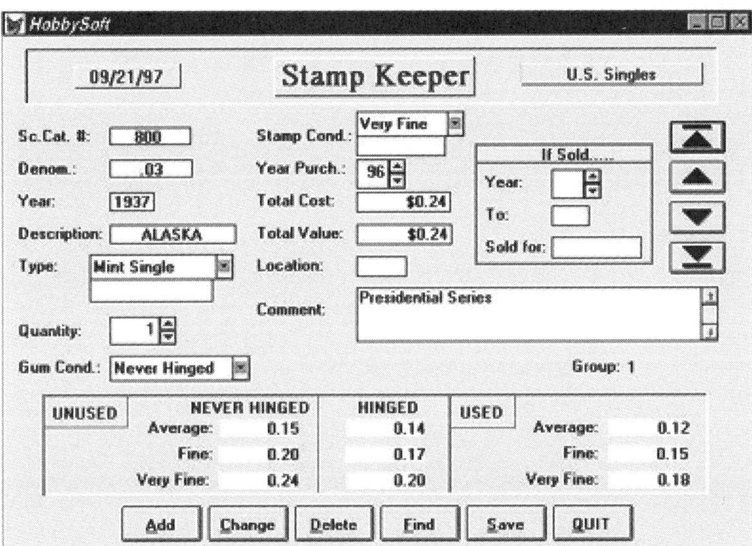

HobbySoft

Written for: DOS, Windows and Macintosh
Database included: yes
Annual updates: yes
Stamp images: no
Price: $69.95 plus $5 shipping
Address: Ninga Software
    882 Pepin Crescent
    Victoria, BC, Canada V8Z 6V6
Phone: orders: (800) 656-4642;
    info: (403) 283-2772
E-mail: scurf@netcom.ca
Internet: www.islandnet.com/~ninga
One-line summary: most flexible report-generation capability of any program

	superb (1.00)	very fine (0.80)	fine (0.60)	average (0.40)	poor (0)	value
documentation (20)	•					20
access speed (10)		•				8
ease of use (10)	•					10
readability (10)		•				8
room for notes (5)	•					5
allows duplication (5)	•					5
customization (10)			•			6
reporting (10)	•					10
ease of installation (10)	•					10
after-sale support (10)	•					10
overall value (100)						92

MyStamps

This bargain offering is a straightforward text-based program that allows you to create a single list of your stamp holdings. There's no printed documentation, but an online manual explains the operations quite well.

The program can track up to 10,000 entries. You enter the Scott number, year issued, category, title, description, face value, comments and key phrases for each item in your list. You can leave any of these fields blank. Once you've entered several records, you can display a list sorted by catalog number, year of issue, category or value. You can get printed output of either the entire sorted list, selected items or just the item currently shown on screen. If you choose to print the entire list, you can either print a quick list, where each entry is printed in one row (42 entries per page), or an expanded list, where all available information from each entry is printed (three items per page).

One limitation of the program is that you can only create one list. You could get around this problem, if necessary, by placing a second copy of MyStamps in another directory on your hard disk and creating another data file in that location. The program is fewer than 45,000 bytes in size.

RAD also offers other programs for collectors of music, videos, books, magazines, coins and cards. There's even a program titled "MyStuff."

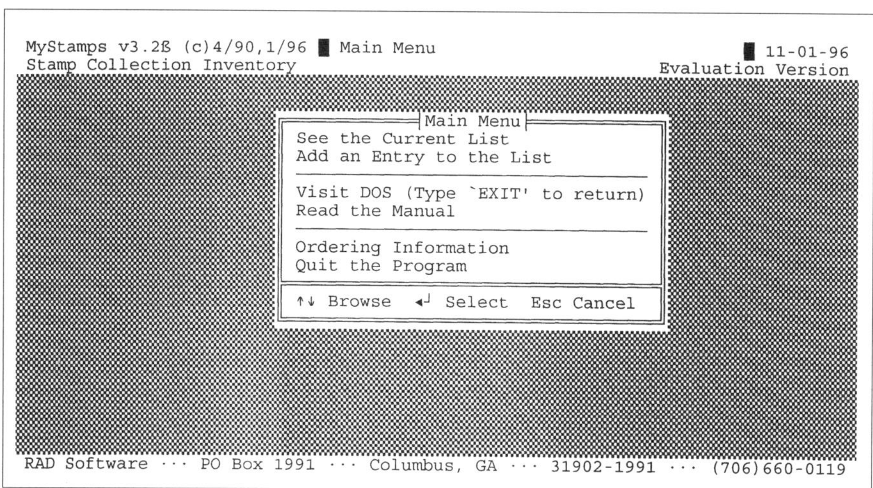

MyStamps

Written for: DOS
Database included: no
Annual updates: no
Stamp images: no
Price: $10
Address: RAD Software
    Rad Delaroderie
    P.O. Box 1991
    Columbus, GA 31902
Phone: (706) 660-0119
E-mail: radiv@aol.com
Internet: members.aol.com/radiv
One-line summary: at $10, the price is right

	superb (1.00)	very fine (0.80)	fine (0.60)	average (0.40)	poor (0)	value
documentation (20)				•		8
access speed (10)	•					10
ease of use (10)	•					10
readability (10)			•			8
room for notes (5)				•		3
allows duplication (5)	•					5
customization (10)					•	4
reporting (10)					•	4
ease of installation (10)	•					10
after-sale support (10)	•					10
overall value (100)						72

Organize Your Collection

This program ships with a 94-page spiral-bound manual, the best documentation in this group. For those users in a hurry, there's a two-page shortcut section with paragraphs briefly explaining how to use the software.

PSG-Homecraft suggests backing up the program disk before proceeding. For a $10 charge, it offers to replace the disk if you damage or lose it. Besides stamps, the program provides formats for 19 other collectibles, including music, coins, books, video tapes, home inventory, sports cards, tokens, wines, model railroads, art, comic books, fabrics and plants.

Although the manual is thorough, you'll want to print out the two-page text file that describes the fields for the stamp-collecting catalog. As shipped, the program provides for catalog number, country, denomination, year issued, description, type, condition, gum condition, comment, storage location, year purchased, quantity, cost and date sold. You can also add a memo field for more detailed comments, such as how you acquired your inverted airmail stamp, a bitmap image of your stamp or a sound file. You can delete unneeded fields and add more fields as desired. If you add a bitmap image, it will be displayed on the data-entry page for that stamp as a thumbnail sketch. Click your mouse on the small picture to display a much larger image.

Various searching and reporting capabilities are provided. You can cross-reference the country and description fields to find all the Christmas stamps issued by Australia. The variety of customization features may seem overwhelming at first, but once you learn how to navigate and select among various menus, you can set up an inventory listing that suits your individual purposes.

Organize Your Collection

Written for: Windows and DOS
Database included: no
Annual updates: no
Stamp images: yes, supplied by user in bitmap format only
Price: $39.95 for DOS version, $59.95 for Windows plus $6 shipping
Address: PSG-HomeCraft Software
P.O. Box 974, Tualatin, OR 97062
Phone: (503) 692-3732
E-mail: HomeCraft@renpdx.com
Internet: www.homecraft.com
One-line summary: easily customized; can be extended for other collectibles

	superb (1.00)	very fine (0.80)	fine (0.60)	average (0.40)	poor (0)	value
documentation (20)	•					20
access speed (10)	•					10
ease of use (10)	•					10
readability (10)		•				8
room for notes (5)	•					5
allows duplication (5)	•					5
customization (10)	•					10
reporting (10)		•				8
ease of installation (10)	•					10
after-sale support (10)	•					10
overall value (100)						96

Philatelic Assistant

Philatelic Assistant (PA) is a no-frills Windows program that allows you to set up an inventory listing of your stamps readily, search through it easily, and print detail or index reports. The index report displays a line-by-line listing of the item number, description of the stamp, its face value and its location. Reports can either be printed or displayed in an on-screen window. You can create multiple files, if desired.

You can't change the fields included in the program, but except for the required item number entry, which must be unique for each stamp, you can leave fields blank. Searching is done through a browse screen; you can specify which stamps are to be displayed based on any combination of style, country, category, condition, year issued, storage location or purchase source. The typical item-number entry would be the Scott number. If you need additional entries for the same stamp, the PA manual suggests you use a numbered suffix after the catalog number.

You can add your own stamp images to stamp records in a wide variety of graphic formats. The images are not displayed with the data-entry screen, but if you click on the "View Stamp" button, a pop-up picture of your stamp will appear.

The manual includes setup instructions and explains the use of the various menu commands. A glossary of computer terms is provided.

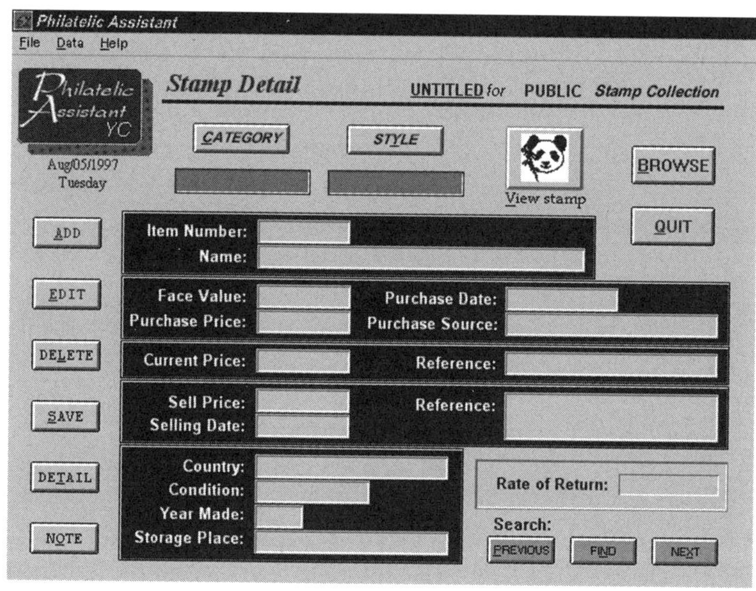

Philatelic Assistant

Written for: Windows

Database included: no, but add-on U.S. database with Scott numbers available for $15

Annual updates: no

Stamp images: yes, supplied by user in a variety of formats

Price: $24.95

Address: AVID Communications
3 Luger Road
Denville, NJ 07830

Phone: (201) 625-7350

One-line summary: a no-frills inventory program with excellent search tools

	superb (1.00)	very fine (0.80)	fine (0.60)	average (0.40)	poor (0)	value
documentation (20)		•				16
access speed (10)	•					10
ease of use (10)	•					10
readability (10)	•					10
room for notes (5)					no	0
allows duplication (5)		•				4
customization (10)				•		4
reporting (10)				•		4
ease of installation (10)	•					10
after-sale support (10)		•				8
overall value (100)						76

ProStamp

ProStamp is a DOS-based spreadsheet program specifically designed for tracking a stamp collection. Each row in the spreadsheet contains information about a specific stamp. Each column lists a particular characteristic of that stamp. The columns correspond to fields in a database; the rows, to records. Column headings include catalog number, description, country, issue date, face value, acquisition date, type, condition, number owned, total purchase price and market value. You enter values for these items as desired. You can leave any of the fields blank. The program also calculates a total value and percentage increase, which are displayed in columns to the right. Finally there's a comment column, limited to 20 characters. You can create more than one spreadsheet if you have multiple collections. A sample spreadsheet is provided.

The manual is provided on disk; you can view it on screen or print it out — it takes about 40 pages. If you are familiar with the DOS version of Lotus 1-2-3, you will have no trouble navigating through the menu choices. The F1 key or Alt-H key combination brings up abbreviated help screens that provide useful information. You can sort the spreadsheet based on a variety of fields. You can print out the entire sheet, a selected range of stamps, or missing stamps, i.e., where the number owned is blank.

This program will run on any DOS machine running DOS 2.1 or larger. It will run on machines with limited amounts of memory, but you can't put 3,000 stamps into a worksheet unless you have at least 525k available memory. If you have less memory than this available, you can still use the program by setting the maximum number of records to a lower value.

```
Pro~Stamp  (1.8)| Alt:  File  Add  Type  Condition  Sort  Options  Help (F1)
    7| Santa Fe
                                                                    |Ready|
Catalog/                         |Issue|Face |  Acq.|
Scott # |Description             Country|Mo Yr|Value|Mo Yr|    Type      |Condition
    3001 Hope                    hungary  9 86           2 87 Single Stamp Mint Fine
     479 Moon and Geese          japan   11 49          10 88 Single Stamp Mint Fine
     425 (e) Rose Red BP of 6    usa        14 0.01      3 88 Booklet Pane Mint Fine
     561 Jefferson               usa        23 0.09     12 86 Single Stamp Used Avg.
    1410 Anti Pollution          usa        70 0.06      8 85 Setenant     NH Fine
     751 Parks                   usa        34 0.01      6 89 Souvenir Sht NH Fine
     944 Santa Fe                usa        46 0.03     10 86 Plate Block  NH Fine
     734 General Kosciuozko      usa        33 0.05      4 87 Single Stamp Mint Avg.
    1425 Blood Donor             usa        71 0.06      3 84 Plate Block  Mint Fine
    1759 Viking Space Mission    usa        78 0.15      6 89 Plate Block  Mint Avg.
    1953 States                  usa        82 0.20     12 88 Sheet        Mint Fine
    2123 School Bus              usa        86 0.03     12 88 Coil Strip 3 Mint Fine
    2201 Stamp Collecting        usa        86 0.22      9 89 Booklet Pane Mint Avg.




Copyright 1989-95 Rob Smetana| Purchase:              Market:
```

ProStamp

Written for: DOS
Database included: no
Annual updates: no
Stamp images: no
Price: $29 plus $4 shipping
Address: Rob Smetana
    Pro~Formance
    132 Alpine Terrace
    San Francisco, CA 94117
Phone: (417) 863-0530
E-mail: Rob-Smetana@worldnet.att.net
One-line summary: fine spreadsheet of inventory program

	superb (1.00)	very fine (0.80)	fine (0.60)	average (0.40)	poor (0)	value
documentation (20)		•				16
access speed (10)	•					10
ease of use (10)	•					10
readability (10)		•				8
room for notes (5)				•		2
allows duplication (5)	•					5
customization (10)			•			6
reporting (10)			•			6
ease of installation (10)	•					10
after-sale support (10)	•					10
overall value (100)						83

StampBase

You'll want to read at least the introductory part of the StampBase manual before starting, since opening or creating a database isn't intuitive. You must select "Records Update" from the opening screen before you can work with any stamp information. You create a personal database covering the stamps you own. Optionally, you can then work with a catalog database supplied by Changing Seasons. Data entry is easy; drop-down lists are provided for category, grade and condition. You can add a stamp image in bitmap or WMF format to any record in the database.

You can sort your records by any combination of fields or search records with various combinations of query commands. Inventory and analysis reports are available. You can create customized reports by just using mouse clicks on a dialog box.

Database catalogs, including Scott numbers, are available for the United States, United Nations, Israel, Germany, Australia, Hong Kong, Japan, China and Canada. The U.S. database contains more than 6,700 market values.

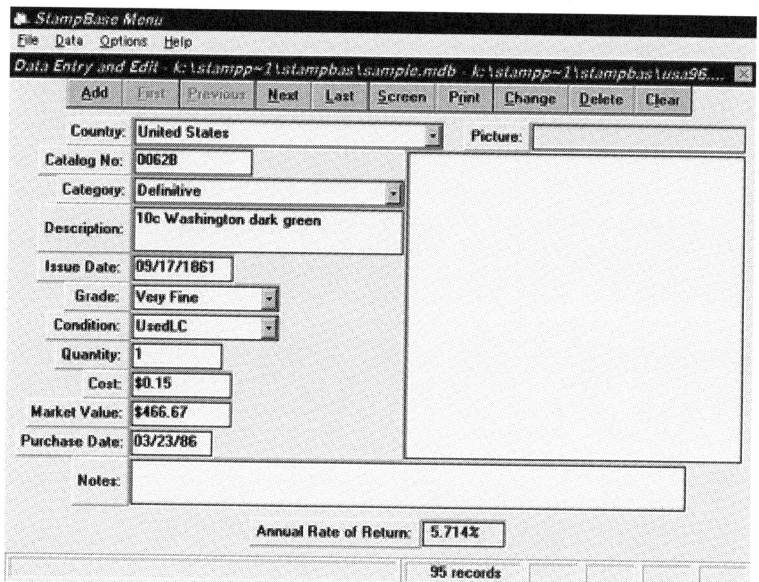

StampBase

Written for: Windows
Database included: sold separately for $20
Annual updates: yes
Stamp images: can be added by user
Price: $34.95 plus $3 shipping
Address: Mark Hetzel
    Changing Seasons Software
    5881 Roanoke Drive
    Madison, WI 53719
Phone orders: (800) 260-2739
    info: (608) 273-2739
E-mail: 71371.731@compuserve.com
One-line summary: easy sort and query
    options; very flexible report capability

	superb (1.00)	very fine (0.80)	fine (0.60)	average (0.40)	poor (0)	value
documentation (20)	•					20
access speed (10)	•					10
ease of use (10)		•				8
readability (10)		•				8
room for notes (5)		•				4
allows duplication (5)	•					5
customization (10)				•		6
reporting (10)				•		4
ease of installation (10)	•					10
after-sale support (10)	•					10
overall value (100)						85

Stamp Collector's Data Base

Roger Edelman's instruction manual provides a friendly first-person introduction to Stamp Collector's Data Base. At 52 pages, the manual is just the right length to explain the use of the program. Edelman includes screen shots for various parts of the program, as well as printouts showing sample reports that can be generated.

The U.S. database included with the basic program contains about 6,000 stamps, including revenues, ducks, postal cards and officials and is based on Scott numbers. You create entries for the stamps you own, but the descriptive and pricing information comes from the built-in database. The group-entry feature lets you enter data about a group of consecutively numbered stamps as long as the condition and quantity of stamps remains the same. You'd use this approach for 50-stamp sheets, such as State Flags or Flowers, rather than entering information about each stamp.

Four types of reports are available for each category of stamps: mint singles, used singles, blocks of four, plate blocks and line pairs/PNCs. All reports can be printed as full reports, inventory lists or want lists.

Additional databases are available for United Nations, Canada and Israel stamps for $25 each.

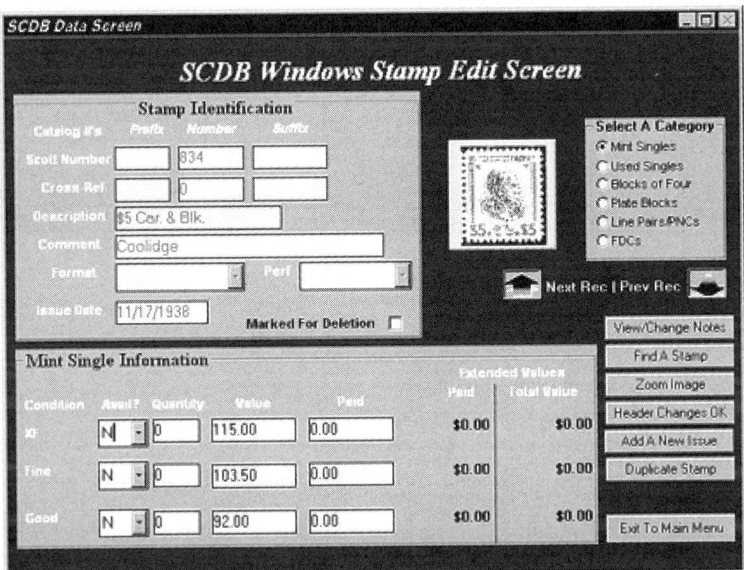

Stamp Collector's Data Base

Written for: DOS and Windows
Database included: yes
Annual updates: yes
Stamp images: CD-ROM available for
    Windows program
Price: $75
Address: Roger Edelman
    8585 River Rock Terrace, Suite B
    Bethesda, MD 20817
Phone orders: (800) 321-SCDB
    info: (301) 320-2451
E-mail: 71570.2065@compuserve.com
One-line summary: thorough, complete
    program available since 1984

	superb (1.00)	very fine (0.80)	fine (0.60)	average (0.40)	poor (0)	value
documentation (20)	•					20
access speed (10)	•					10
ease of use (10)		•				8
readability (10)		•				8
room for notes (5)	•					5
allows duplication (5)	•					5
customization (10)				•		6
reporting (10)	•					10
ease of installation (10)	•					10
after-sale support (10)	•					10
overall value (100)						92

Stamp Master GB

In the true British tradition, Stamp Master GB is a thorough and demanding DOS-based inventory program. A Windows version, including stamp images, is available.

You'll have to consult the manual to find out all the possible features included. Each screen in the program is identified with a number. Most of the manual is devoted to an explanation of the various screens. The menu route to each screen is shown, the purpose of the screen is stated, and field descriptions/possible entries are listed. A short summary in the front of the manual describes the program structure, which is divided into two parts: the stamp-details database and the user's collection record. Basic tasks are described in Section 6 of the manual. I'd suggest reading this section before examining the detailed screen descriptions.

You can modify exchange rates in the program so you can track the value of your stamps in current dollars (or any other currency) rather than pounds. You can change the screen colors, choose a date format and optionally use a password at startup.

A variety of reports are available, including user collection, value reports, collection statistics, want lists and results of searches.

Stamp Master GB includes National Postal Museum data on stamps with detailed information on each stamp, year data and information on the *NPM Chronolist*. *Chronolist* numbers are used to identify the stamps in the database, since Stanley Gibbons has not licensed the use of its catalog numbers to software vendors. A user reference field is provided for you to identify your stamps, using any catalog system or your own terminology. You can create reports sorted on this field.

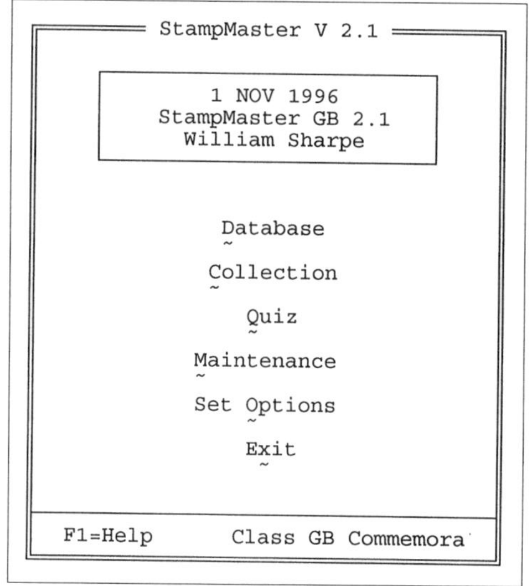

Stamp Master GB

Written for: DOS and Windows
Database included: yes Annual updates: yes
Stamp images: no
Price: £50, approx. $75 for DOS and Windows database, £75, approx. $112 for CD-ROM with database and images
Address: Philatelic Software Ltd.
Valley View, Coleman's Lane
Nazeing, Essex EN9 2EA, England
Phone: 44 992 89 3086
E-mail: 100657.2272@compuserve.com
Internet: ourworld.compuserve.com/ homepages/philsoft
One-line summary: a must for British collectors

	superb (1.00)	very fine (0.80)	fine (0.60)	average (0.40)	poor (0)	value
documentation (20)	•					20
access speed (10)	•					10
ease of use (10)		•				8
readability (10)		•				8
room for notes (5)	•					5
allows duplication (5)		•				4
customization (10)			•			6
reporting (10)	•					10
ease of installation (10)	•					10
after-sale support (10)		•				8
overall value (100)						89

StampPro

This inexpensive Windows program includes a database of U.S. stamps, including Scott numbers. The manual is a short five-page text file that you'll want to print out, since it includes a brief tutorial on how to use the program.

A database of U.S. stamps is built into the program. You can add information from this database to your personal database and then modify it as desired. You don't have to fill in information for each field. A notes field is provided, allowing for comments up to 250 characters about each stamp. There's a group-entry feature for entering information about a series of stamps instead of one at a time. The only search capability is by catalog number. You type the catalog number in the correct field box, then click on the magnifying-glass button to display the record for that stamp.

There are limited report capabilities for inventory, want lists or missing stamps. You can then export the report to a variety of other formats (including Excel, Quattro Pro and Lotus 1-2-3 spreadsheets) and operate on the resulting data in another program.

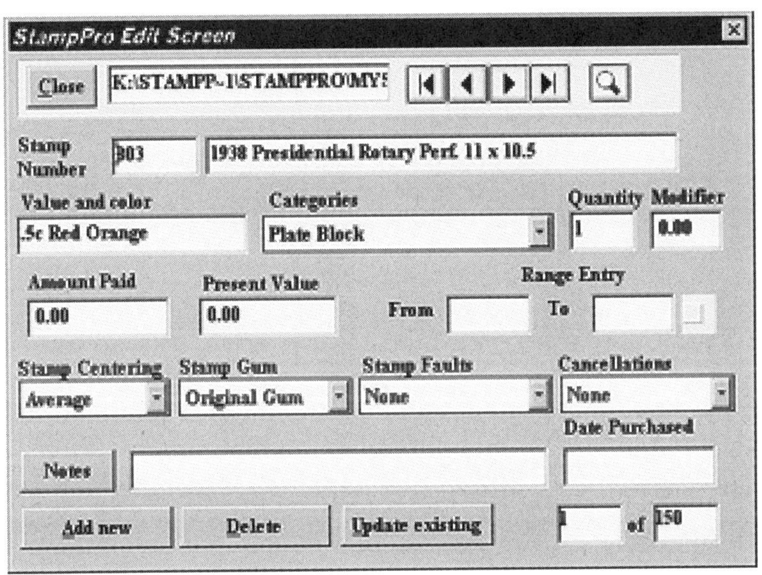

StampPro

Written for: Windows
Database included: yes   Annual updates: no
Stamp images: no
Price: $20
Address: Franklin Leibsly
    MMR Software
    P.O. Box 34916
    Bethesda, MD 20827
Phone: (301) 493-4421
E-mail: help@mmrsoft.com
Sales: sales@mmrsoft.com
Internet: www.mmrsoft.com
One-line summary: lowest-priced program that includes a database

	superb (1.00)	very fine (0.80)	fine (0.60)	average (0.40)	poor (0)	value
documentation (20)				•		8
access speed (10)	•					10
ease of use (10)		•				8
readability (10)		•				8
room for notes (5)		•				4
allows duplication (5)	•					5
customization (10)			•			6
reporting (10)				•		4
ease of installation (10)	•					10
after-sale support (10)	•					10
overall value (100)						73

Scott Stamps of the United States

Here's essentially the U.S. portion of Scott *Standard Postage Stamp Catalogue* Volume 1 with a few extra features. The CD-ROM includes a listing and color images of all U.S. stamps in the following categories: postage, airpost, airpost special delivery, special delivery, registration, certified mail, postage due, offices in China, Official, parcel post, parcel post postage due, special handling, revenue and hunting permit.

In the Stamp View mode, you can look up stamps by Scott number or by year issued. The stamp image is shown on the left of your screen, with details about the stamp displayed on the right. You can easily navigate to previous or succeeding Scott numbers or years by using the appropriate arrows near the top right of the screen. You can also enter a Scott number or year to display information about other stamps.

You can print out the stamp image and detailed information about each stamp. Should you decide to print out everything, be forewarned that you will have more than 4,000 pages, since each stamp entry prints out on a separate page.

The interactive features of the program include the creation of lists for stamps you hold (a collection list) or expect to buy (a want list). You can add stamps to either category from the Stamp View mode or switch to either the Want List or Collection List mode to see a line-by-line listing of your stamps. The program also includes most of the background information about stamps contained in the paper catalog as well as a Scott product guide.

Installation is straightforward. If you plan to use the program only as a look-up catalog, you can run it directly from your CD-ROM drive. If you want to create collection or want lists, you need to copy several files from the CD-ROM to your hard disk. These files take up about 4 megabytes of space.

I received a prerelease version of this program, which did not include a manual or a help system. Since these important features are lacking in this preliminary version, I did not create a chart for this program as I did with the other software programs listed in this chapter.

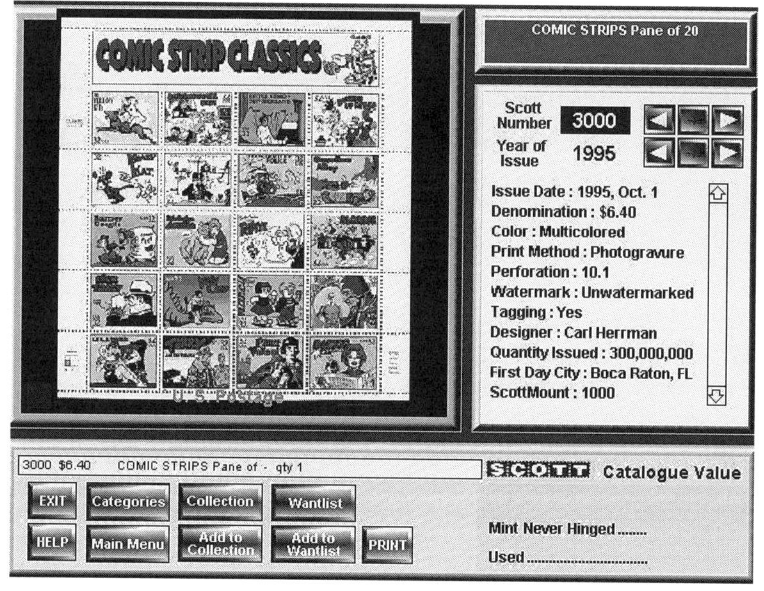

Scott Stamps of the United States

Written for: Windows
Database included: yes
Annual updates: planned
Stamp images: included with program, can be printed out
Price: not yet determined
Address: Scott Publishing Company
    911 Vandemark Road
    P.O. Box 828
    Sidney, Ohio 45365
Phone: (937) 498-0802
Internet: www.csmonline.com/scott
One-line summary: Excellent stamp images, simple but effective
    collection and want list input.

Inventory Program Ranking

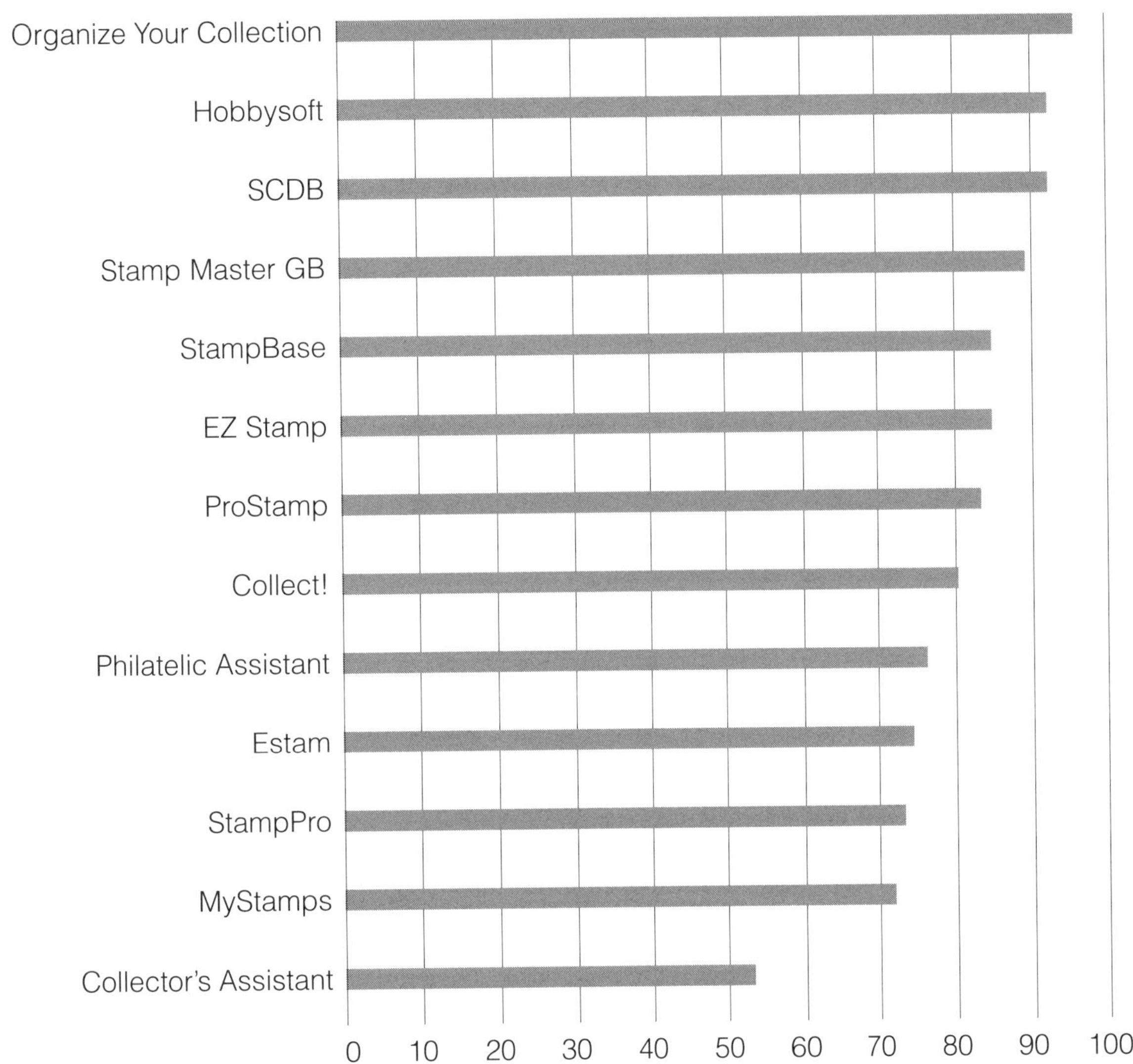

Chapter 3

Sorting

Putting Your Stamps in Order

Simply Sorting

You can use the SORT command in DOS as a very simple and cheap way to keep track of your stamps. All you need to do is create a listing using a text editor, such as the DOS Edit program or Windows Notepad. Put all the information about each stamp on one line. Use the TAB key to line up the various fields, or specific pieces of information, in columns. Hit the ENTER key at the end of each line. Save the file with an appropriate name. Keep the line length to fewer than 80 characters to avoid a con-fusing display when the line wraps past the 80-character limit displayed on screen.

I've shown a sample input text field named PARPOST.LST below. Note the extra zeros in the catalog numbers. These are required for proper sorting.

You can put the listing in sorted order on screen with the following command at your DOS prompt: SORT PARPOST.LST

This command sorts the list numerically based on the first column of your file, which is the beginning of the catalog number, displaying the following listing on your screen:

```
                    PARPOST.LST

    PP04   0.04   Rural Carrier                         1912
    PP05   0.05   Mail Train and Mail Bag on Rack       1912
    PP06   0.10   Steamship "Kronsprinz Wilhelm"        1912
    PP07   0.15   Automobile Service                    1912
    PP08   0.20   Airplane Carrying Mail                1912
    PP09   0.25   Manufacturing                         1912
    PP11   0.75   Harvesting                            1912
    PP02   0.02   City Carrier                          1912
    PP01   0.01   Post Office Clerk                     1912
    PP12   1.00   Fruit Growing                         1913
    PP03   0.03   Railway Postal Clerk                  1913
    PP10   0.50   Dairying                              1913
```

```
                  SORT PARPOST.LST

    PP01   0.01   Post Office Clerk                     1912
    PP02   0.02   City Carrier                          1912
    PP03   0.03   Railway Postal Clerk                  1913
    PP04   0.04   Rural Carrier                         1912
    PP05   0.05   Mail Train and Mail Bag on Rack       1912
    PP06   0.10   Steamship "Kronsprinz Wilhelm"        1912
    PP07   0.15   Automobile Service                    1912
    PP08   0.20   Airplane Carrying Mail                1912
    PP09   0.25   Manufacturing                         1912
    PP10   0.50   Dairying                              1913
    PP11   0.75   Harvesting                            1912
    PP12   1.00   Fruit Growing                         1913
```

```
                    SORT PARPOST.LST | MORE
PP08     0.20     Airplane Carrying Mail              1912
PP07     0.15     Automobile Service                  1912
PP02     0.02     City Carrier                        1912
PP10     0.50     Dairying                            1913
PP12     1.00     Fruit Growing                       1913
PP11     0.75     Harvesting                          1912
PP05     0.05     Mail Train and Mail Bag on Rack     1912
PP09     0.25     Manufacturing                       1912
PP01     0.01     Post Office Clerk                   1912
PP03     0.03     Railway Postal Clerk                1913
PP04     0.04     Rural Carrier                       1912
PP06     0.10     Steamship "Kronsprinz Wilhelm"      1912
```

```
                    FIND "Carrier" PARPOST

——————————— parpost.lst
PP04     0.04     Rural Carrier                       1912
PP02     0.02     City Carrier                        1912
```

If the top of your listing scrolls off the screen, as it will if it's longer than about 20 lines, you can add a pipe symbol (the vertical bar) and the DOS filter "MORE" to your command line, as shown below, to display a screenful of information at one time. DOS will wait for you to hit any key to continue with your listing.

SORT PARPOST.LST | MORE

If you want to save your sorted listing, just add a file name to your command, preceded by a ">" or redirection symbol. You won't see the sorted listing on screen, but you will create a text file that contains the listing.

You don't have to sort your list based only on the first column of your file. If you want to sort alphabetically based on the description of your stamp, use the command SORT /+21 PARPOST.LST > DESCRPT.SRT.

This command tells DOS to sort the listing starting with column 21, which is where the description of your stamps starts in your file, and store the results in a file named DESCRPT.SRT. The sorted file is shown above:

Another DOS command, FIND, will search through your text file and retrieve those lines that contain certain text. For example, to display only those stamps that contain "Carrier" in the records of your stamp listing, you'd enter the command FIND "Carrier" PARPOST

You'd see the display shown above on screen:

Note that you must place quotation marks around the text string that you are looking for. Also, the text search is case-sensitive; if you entered "carrier" as your search string, FIND would not locate the above lines in the file. You can send the results of this command to another file by adding the redirection symbol and another file name to this command.

You can type SORT /? or FIND /? at the DOS prompt to find out more information about how to use these commands. You can also type HELP SORT or HELP FIND at the DOS prompt (except in a Windows 95 MS-DOS window) to display detailed information.

In versions of DOS earlier than 6.0, there's a limit to the size of file that SORT and FIND can handle. You'll get an error message when the text file is larger than about 64,000 characters. Also, earlier DOS versions may require using two redirection symbols in your SORT commands, such as SORT < PARPOST.LST >SORTED.LST

This command tells DOS to use the SORT command on the first file name and direct the sorted output to the second file name.

Sorting with Word

You can use a word processor as a means of tracking your stamp inventory as long as your requirements aren't too demanding. Most word processors include a table feature, which lets you set up rows and columns for orderly entry of your information. Each row in the table contains information about one stamp (or set of stamps); each column includes specific information about that stamp, such as year of issue, denomination, color, catalog value or purchase price. The intersection of a row and column is called a cell, just as in a spreadsheet.

The table can be as large as desired, but if you plan to print results, you are limited to the maximum width that your printer can handle. If you have a particularly long entry in one row, you can wrap that cell's text to use additional lines in the printout. Note that catalog value and catalog number are multiple-line entries in the following tables.

You don't need to enter data in any particular order. Most word processors include a sorting command for their tables. For example, you reach a dialog box with various sorting options from the Table Sort menu command in Microsoft Word for Windows. You can sort on one, two or three columns in either ascending or descending order. You can specify whether your table has a header row, that is, a row of titles or column headings. If so, you don't want to include the header row in the sort.

I've included a short table of information about some of the Famous Americans issues. The first table shows the entries I originally made. The second table is the result I get when I sort the table by category and then by name in alphabetical order. The third table is the result of sorting by catalog value in descending order, i.e., highest catalog value first, then by catalog number.

Table as Entered

CatalogNo	Category	Name	Denom	CatalogValue	YearIssued
881	Composers	Herbert	0.03	0.15	1940
880	Composers	Sousa	0.02	0.15	1940
891	Inventors	McCormick	0.03	0.15	1940
893	Inventors	Bell	0.10	10.00	1940
889	Inventors	Whitney	0.01	0.15	1940
888	Artists	Remington	0.10	1.75	1940
887	Artists	French	0.05	0.48	1940
884	Artists	Stuart	0.01	0.15	1940
878	Scientists	Addams	0.10	1.00	1940
873	Educators	Washington	0.10	1.10	1940
870	Educators	Hopkins	0.02	0.15	1940
868	Poets	Riley	0.10	1.65	1940

Table sorted by category, then by name

CatalogNo	Category	Name	Denom	CatalogValue	YearIssued
887	Artists	French	0.05	0.48	1940
888	Artists	Remington	0.10	1.75	1940
884	Artists	Stuart	0.01	0.15	1940
881	Composers	Herbert	0.03	0.15	1940
880	Composers	Sousa	0.02	0.15	1940
870	Educators	Hopkins	0.02	0.15	1940
873	Educators	Washington	0.10	1.10	1940
893	Inventors	Bell	0.10	10.00	1940
891	Inventors	McCormick	0.03	0.15	1940
889	Inventors	Whitney	0.01	0.15	1940
868	Poets	Riley	0.10	1.65	1940
878	Scientists	Addams	0.10	1.00	1940

Table sorted by descending catalog value, then by catalog number

CatalogNo	Category	Name	Denom	CatalogValue	YearIssued
893	Inventors	Bell	0.10	10.00	1940
888	Artists	Remington	0.10	1.75	1940
868	Poets	Riley	0.10	1.65	1940
873	Educators	Washington	0.10	1.10	1940
878	Scientists	Addams	0.10	1.00	1940
887	Artists	French	0.05	0.48	1940
870	Educators	Hopkins	0.02	0.15	1940
880	Composers	Sousa	0.02	0.15	1940
881	Composers	Herbert	0.03	0.15	1940
884	Artists	Stuart	0.01	0.15	1940
889	Inventors	Whitney	0.01	0.15	1940
891	Inventors	McCormick	0.03	0.15	1940
			Total	**$16.88**	

I added a last row to the final table (after I sorted it) to provide a total catalog value for this list. I placed my cursor in the catalog-value cell in the last row and chose Table Formula from Word's menu.

The dialog box suggested using the formula =SUM(ABOVE), which is just what I wanted. The dialog box also offered various formats for the results. I chose dollars and cents.

One caveat when working with any sort routine: Save your document before you sort so you can easily retrieve the original arrangement if the results of your sort are not what you expected. Word includes an Undo feature that should achieve the same result.

There's not much point in using the Find feature for this short table, but you can locate any table entry by using the dialogue box from the Edit Find menu command. If I typed in "Hopkins," Word would highlight the "Hopkins" found in the next to last row of the first table.

You can take advantage of the word processor's formatting features to make your table attractive for screen display and printout. Note that the column headings are in boldface and centered, the catalog numbers are centered in the first column, and the currency values are right-justified. You can also use the copy-and-paste feature to reduce the amount of typing required. I only typed in "1940" once.

Although I've used Microsoft Word for the above example, most contemporary word-processing programs for DOS, Windows and Macintosh computers have similar features. If you own one of these word processors, you may find a cheap and easy solution to your inventory needs. You'll need to move on to spreadsheets or databases, though, if your needs are more complex.

Spreadsheet Sorting with Excel

You can sort spreadsheet information in the same manner as a word-processing document, with sort order based on one, two or three columns.

Microsoft Excel and other Windows or Macintosh spreadsheets include database functions that readily display customized information about your stamps. The following Excel spreadsheet contains the same information I used in Microsoft Word. I didn't retype this information for the spreadsheet. I used Edit Copy in Word to copy my table to the Windows clipboard, then used Edit Paste in a blank Excel spreadsheet to put the information there. I changed column widths, modified the font size of my text, and formatted the denomination and catalog-value columns as numbers instead of text.

Excel includes a Data menu item. The first entry on this menu is sorting with the same choices that Word provides. The second entry is filtering, which displays selected information from my spreadsheet based on the criteria I enter. When I select Data Filter from the Excel menu, I get a submenu to turn on autofiltering. When I choose this option, Excel displays a drop-down arrow in each column heading. Clicking on one of these arrows brings up a listing of all the different entries for this column. For example, if I click on the drop-down box in the Catergory column, I can

	A	B	C	D	E	F
1	Catalog No.	Category	Name	Denom.	Catalog Value	Year Issued
2	881	Composers	Herbert	0.03		1940
3	880	Composers	Sousa	0.02		1940
4	891	Inventors	McCormick	0.03		1940
5	893	Inventors	Bell	0.10		1940
6	889	Inventors	Whitney	0.01		1940
7	888	Artists	Remington	0.10	1.75	1940
8	887	Artists	French	0.05	0.48	1940
9	884	Artists	Stuart	0.01	0.15	1940
10	878	Scientists	Addams	0.10	1.00	1940
11	873	Educators	Washington	0.10	1.10	1940
12	870	Educators	Hopkins	0.02	0.15	1940
13	868	Poets	Riley	0.10	1.65	1940

Unfiltered spreadsheet with drop-down box selected

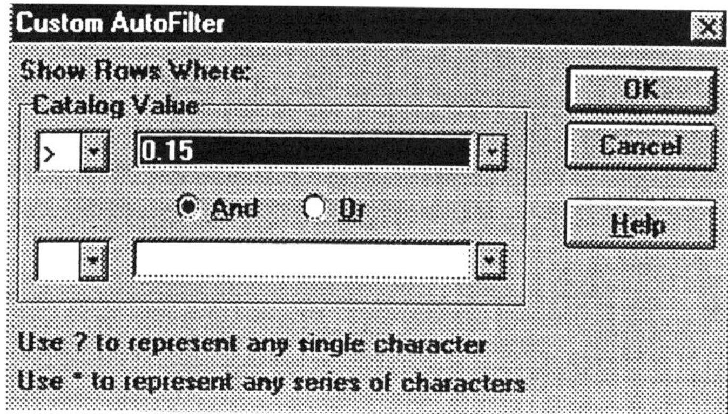

	A	B	C	D	E	F
1	**Catalog No.**	**Categor**	**Name**	**Denom**	**Catalog Value**	**Year Issued**
5	893	Inventors	Bell	0.10	10.00	1940
7	888	Artists	Remington	0.10	1.75	1940
8	887	Artists	French	0.05	0.48	1940
10	878	Scientists	Addams	0.10	1.00	1940
11	873	Educators	Washington	0.10	1.10	1940
13	868	Poets	Riley	0.10	1.65	1940

Filtered spreadsheet with catalog values above 15¢

Custom filtering dialogue box for above spreadsheet

choose Composers, Inventors, Artists, Scientists or Poets. When I select Artists, for example, Excel will display only those rows or records that contain the word Artists in that column. The remaining rows are still in the spreadsheet; they are hidden from view.

You can combine criteria from more than one column to get, for example, a listing of stamps in the Artists category where the denomination is 0.01 (1¢). This is not too useful, since you know there's only one stamp there. You can also create a custom criteria by choosing the custom item from the drop-down list for catalog value. That choice brings up a custom autofilter dialogue box, where, for example, you can set the criteria to values that are greater than 15¢, i.e., showing all the stamps that have a catalog value above the minimum. Note that the filtered spreadsheet only contains

rows 1 (the headings), 5, 7, 8, 10, 11 and 13.

You can print the filtered spreadsheet directly or copy the information to another area or page in your spreadsheet for future reference.

I've only scratched the surface on the possibilities of organizing your stamp collection with Excel. There's an entire chapter in the user's guide, "Sorting and Filtering Data in a List," that goes into much greater detail. Other spreadsheets provide similar capabilities.

Chapter 4

Databases

Organizing Your Stamps

A database program provides the greatest flexibility possible in arranging the information about your stamps exactly the way you want. You'll have to put up with some complexity to achieve this flexibility, but the latest graphical database programs are relatively easy to learn.

You can get by with just a few terms when you're working with spreadsheets — rows, columns and cells. Database terminology is slightly different. It refers to tables, records and fields. A table looks just like a spreadsheet. It consists of rows and columns. The information in each row is called a record; each column represents a field. A field gives one piece of information about your stamp; for example, its catalog number. Other fields contain additional information, such as denomination, catalog value, year issued and notes. Taken together, these fields make up a record, which is all the information you care to enter about each stamp. All the records together make up a table.

A simple database would consist of just one table, but a database may contain two or more tables that contain related information about your stamps. You could set up one field in your database to identify the dealer from whom you bought your stamp. You could add the dealer's address and phone number as additional fields for this stamp. If you purchase multiple stamps from the dealer, you'd have a lot of duplicate information in your table, since you'd be recording the dealer, his address and his phone number for each stamp. You save entry time, reduce the size of your data files, greatly reduce the possibility of errors and simplify modifications by creating a separate table for dealers' names, addresses and phone numbers. You still would have a dealer entry for your stamp, but if you wanted to check the name or phone number, you'd use the related table, which lists all the dealers with whom you work. If the dealer moves or changes his phone number, you only need to change one entry in the dealer table rather than multiple entries in your stamp table.

Microsoft Access, part of the Microsoft Office Suite for Windows, can serve your database needs whether you're using one or more tables. Other databases have similar capabilities. I used Q&A, a text-based database program, for my Australian stamp collection. Symantec, the publisher of Q&A, brought out a Windows version of the product, but it hasn't sold nearly as well as the databases in the suites provided by the major software companies, Microsoft, Lotus and Corel. Q&A included one feature, the Intelligent Assistant, that allowed the user to type in English-type commands, which was most helpful to occasional database users. You could teach Q&A to recognize the command "Show me all the Prexies" to display your holdings from the 1938 Presidential issue.

You can create a database from scratch in Access or import text, spreadsheet or database files in other formats. The import capability is especially helpful if you already have a typed listing of your stamp holdings. Even if your file format isn't supported, you can usually save your data in your original program as text and then import that information into Access.

If you're starting from scratch, you first set up a table with the names of your field and the data type for each field. You can modify the table at any time, but you should give some thought beforehand as to what information you want to keep track of for your stamps. As shown in Figure 1, I used catalog number, category and name as text fields in my simple example. I used number as the data type for year issued, but I could have used date as well, especially if I wanted to identify the exact date of issue for each stamp. I set denomination and catalog value as currency items. You could include an image of your stamp as a field, assuming you have a graphics file with a picture of the stamp.

Once you have set up the field names, you can start entering data for each of your stamps using a simple table or by creating a form. The form is preferable if you have many fields of information to enter. You may not be able to see all the fields on screen at the same time with table entry. The form provides a window so you see only the entries for one record at a time. Access provides a Form Wizard to assist you in creating a form. One choice is AutoForm, which creates a simple one-column form that lists the field names and provides blocks for you

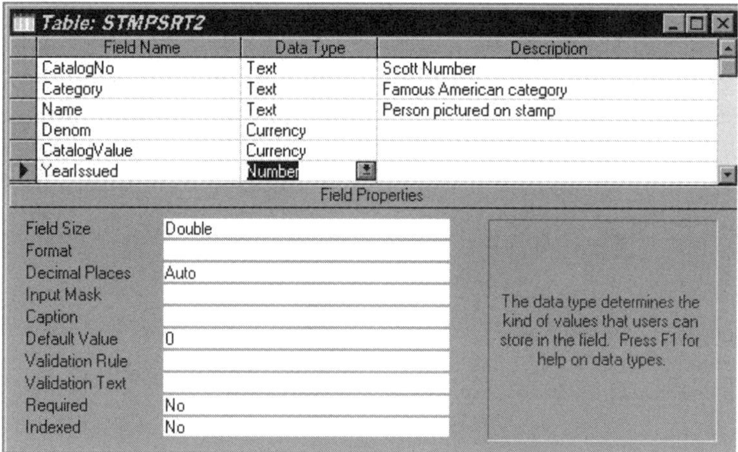

Figure 1.
This example uses catalog number, category and name as text fields.

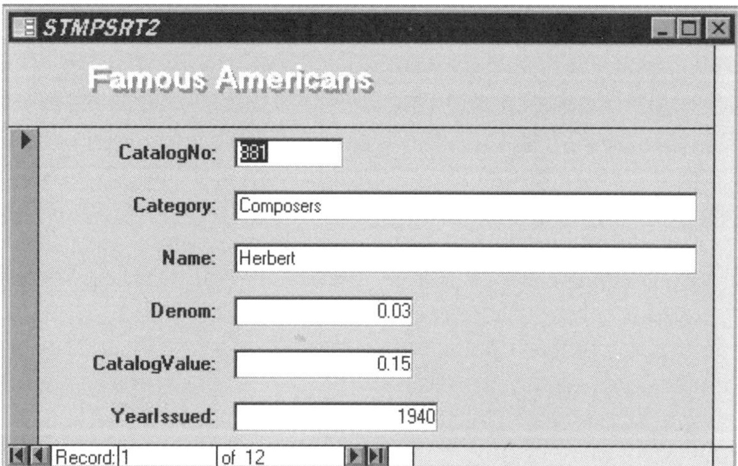

Figure 2.
AutoForm creates a simple one-column form that lists the field names and provides blocks for entering data.

to use for entering data (see Figure 2). The bottom of the form displays a VCR-like box that permits navigation through all the records in your database. The leftmost arrow takes you to the first record; the next arrow moves to the previous record. The arrows on the right move the cursor to the next and last record, respectively.

To start, there's only a blank record displayed. You enter data in each field by typing, then move to the next field by using the Enter or Tab key. You can also use the mouse to click on a field's data area. Once you've entered data in the last field on the form, hitting the Enter key will move you to a new blank record. You can tell Access to use a default value in one or more fields. For example, since all the Famous Americans stamps were issued in 1940, you could set 1940 as the default value for the Year Issued field. You also can save typing time by using the Control key plus the apostrophe key to insert the value you used in the previous record for that field. In addition, you can set up a pick list, which allows you to choose from a list of entries for a field. If you keep track of perforations, this will save a lot of typing and avoid errors when you need to enter "11½ by 10."

You can create queries to look at stamps that meet certain criteria. You can display all the fields or selected fields in your query results. You can save a complicated query with a name so you can use it again without re-entering all the conditions. You can print the results of your queries, but your formatting possibilities are limited.

Access provides a Report Wizard, which is a series of dialogue boxes that appear on screen to help you design a report output. The wizard takes care of the most difficult parts, but you can modify the results after the wizard has finished running. You can switch between a design view and a print preview to see what your report will look like when you print it. If you are unhappy with the screen preview, just return to the design view and modify it.

As shown in Figure 3, I created a report for showing Famous Americans stamps

Famous Americans by Category and Name

29-Oct-97

CatalogNo	Category	Name	Denom	CatalogValue	YearIssued
887	Artists	French	0.05	0.48	1940
888		Remington	0.10	1.75	1940
884		Stuart	0.01	0.15	1940
881	Composers	Herbert	0.03	0.15	1940
880		Sousa	0.02	0.15	1940
870	Educators	Hopkins	0.02	0.15	1940
873		Washington	0.10	1.10	1940
893	Inventors	Bell	0.10	10.00	1940
891		McCormick	0.03	0.15	1940
889		Whitney	0.01	0.15	1940
868	Poets	Riley	0.10	1.65	1940
878	Scientists	Addams	0.10	1.00	1940
			Total:	**$16.88**	

Figure 3.
This report for the Famous Americans stamps was sorted by category and then by name. The wizard provided the headings.

sorted by category, then by name. The wizard provided the headings, the arrangement of items on the page and the sorting. The wizard also gave me total columns for the denomination, catalog value and year-issued fields. The first and third of these totals are meaningless, so I deleted these totals. By default, the category listings (artists, composers, educators and so on) were repeated in each record. Since I was sorting on these categories, I improved the report's appearance by hiding duplicate listings of the category name.

Chapter 5

Album Pages
Displaying Your Stamps

The second most popular use of computers for stamp collectors is that of preparing album or exhibit pages. As with inventory software, the user has three choices: a dedicated album-page preparation program, a commercial program that he adapts for his purpose, and writing his own program with a programming language. Creating your own album-page design program from scratch is a lot more difficult than creating an inventory program.

What should an album-page-preparation program provide the user? Mike Francis, who has created hundreds of album pages for his own use, sent me an eight-page design guide in 1995 for making your own stamp-album pages. His guide covers a number of issues. I'm not reproducing it entirely here, but Francis provides the most complete discussion of album-page design that I've run across.

You'd think it would be a simple matter to put a border on a piece of paper, a country name at the top of the page, a few mount locations on the page and some associated text with each location. It's not, at least if you desire an aesthetically pleasing result.

Don't try creating album pages just to save the cost of purchasing existing albums, at least not if you value your time. Create album pages for topical collections, specialties, stamp varieties and areas where no preprinted album pages are available. Create album pages for stamps you want to describe in greater detail than standard album pages provide.

Start slowly. Create several draft album pages. Pick one page that stands out above the others, and make that page the foundation for your album pages.

Francis lists several design issues: Are you going to put the country name on each page, just the first page or none of the pages? Pick a font size and type and stick with it throughout your collection. Are you going to include spaces for stamp varieties? Will you place mint and used stamps on the same page or on separate pages? How many stamps do you want to place on each page? What should you do if you don't know the size or orientation of a particular stamp? Francis suggests skipping this page until you find out.

How do you overcome the tedious nature of creating each album page? Eventually, you'll find some pages looking the same as others. Copy the page that's close to what you need, then adjust the new page as necessary. What do you do about incomplete stamp series? Francis decided to wait until the series is complete before creating a page for it. How do you format an album page? You could refer to a similar Scott or Harris page, but Francis suggests laying out your page on your PC screen. You can get eight to 10 large stamps or 16 to 25 smaller stamps on one page if you don't have too much descriptive information.

There are several text issues. First is the choice of font. Francis suggests limiting the different typefaces on a page to two, perhaps a sans-serif font, such as Arial, for the country name, stamp series name and information at the page bottom, and a serif font, such as Times Roman, for stamp descriptions and numbers.

Where do you want to place the stamp number, inside or outside the mount frame? Put it inside the frame if you don't want numbers displayed once the stamp is in place. If you do place text inside the frame, be sure you are using stamp mounts rather than hinges. Ink or toner may transfer to the back of a hinged stamp after time in a closed album.

Where do you want to place descriptive information about the stamp? If you put it inside the mount area, you're limited in the amount of information you can place there plus you can't see it without lifting the stamp. However, note that the more descriptive information you provide, the longer it will take to create your page. You can use abbreviations, but be consistent throughout your pages. Should you include global stamp descriptions on the album page, such as year of issue, or name of the stamp series? Francis votes an emphatic yes, saying that you can never place enough descriptions on the page.

Francis suggests designing a blank template page to start each country collection. Put the country name at the top, and add a border, if desired. Put the name of whatever information you want at the bottom of the page, and include at least one sample of stamp-description text, stamp number and series description in the desired font.

As to pages, Francis suggests using heavy paper, particularly if you are placing a large number of stamps on one page. Ideally you'll want acid-free paper that allows removing stamp hinges without tearing the paper. Use plain white 8½- by 11-inch paper. Ordinary bond or copier paper is too light to support your stamps on the page. Use this type paper for draft copies of your album pages. Better yet, use the print-preview feature available in most Windows software programs, to see what your album page looks like on screen prior to using any paper.

I'd suggest getting the thickest possible paper your printer can handle. Don't go overboard, though. Just because you can feed 90-pound or heavier stock into your printer doesn't mean that your machine will not suffer some damage. You can misalign the feed path and affect subsequent sheets, no matter what thickness. One solution, especially for exhibit pages, is to use 28-pound paper for your pages, then mount each page to a thicker stock sheet. This approach brings up the question of glue and tape. Don't use any self-adhesive material; any glue that's "lickable" is probably inert and OK to use.

Don't put page numbers on each album page unless you are positive you won't be adding additional pages for stamp varieties any place in the collection.

Questions arise about the permanence of the ink or toner used by computer printers. I have printouts from 1983 that have been stored in loose-leaf binders that are as readable today as they were 13 years ago. These weren't album pages; I used plain form-fed computer paper in a dot-matrix printer. When I was using a new printer ribbon, the printout was heavy and did bleed through to the back of the page, but did not show up on adjoining pages in my binder.

Inkjet printing may smear if moisture contacts the page. Don't cry on your stamps! I'd recommend protecting your stamps with stamp mounts rather than hinges on any album pages you create. If you do use hinges, don't print anything inside the frame where you place the stamp; some ink or toner will probably be transferred to the back of your stamp.

In researching information about this chapter, I came across a brief article by W. W. Wagner in the January-February 1968 issue of *First Days*, published by the American First Day Cover Society. Wagner used a GE 400 series computer and an electro-mechanical plotter to generate album pages.

Exhibit Pages

Donald Beuthel prepared what was probably the first exhibit pages related to computers. His exhibit won the grand award at Topex '79, but he had been showing these pages at other shows for over four years before that date. In fact, his exhibit was shown so often that one observer commented that it ought to win some sort of traveling trophy because it had been at every show he had seen in the past two years.

"Computers on Stamps" looked at the historical development of calculating devices, from counting on your fingers to the modern computers of today (1979). Persons such as Leibnitz, Pascal, Da Vinci, Quevedo and Schickard, each of whom had a part in developing calculating machines, are shown as well as the machines themselves.

A second section covered the actual computer and data-processing materials shown on stamps, including punched cards, punched tape, magnetic tape, terminals and consoles.

A third section included computer applications such as computer art and design, graphs and printouts, science, weather and computerized mail handling. A final section showed the special covers and cancellations related to the subject. A page is shown in Figure 4.

Pittpex '92 was the first stamp show that included only exhibit pages prepared with computers. The organizers prepared an *Idea Book* following the show. This document covers a total of 21 exhibits plus four youth exhibits. Nine exhibits were prepared using the Macintosh computer, seven with IBM-compatible equipment, two with a Sun Sparc II computer, two using a Panasonic word processor and one unspecified. Most exhibitors used word-processing programs to display their pages, but desktop publishing, presentation graphics and drawing programs were also represented. Figure 5 is a page from Conrad Bush's exhibit, "The Politics of War," prepared using an IBM compatible 386SX computer, an Oxylaser 400 laser printer and CorelDraw 2.0 software.

Besides the exhibit pages, the document includes several helpful essays. Randy Neil provided a set of guidelines; he pointed out that exhibiting-evaluation rules have not changed. Judges are looking for the stamp and presentation values of an exhibit, not how computer-literate the exhibitor is. He listed some advantages that a computer brings to the task of preparing an exhibit, such as uniformity of style, making tedious artwork easier, learning page layout techniques and the opportunity to experiment with the page layout without wasting paper.

Two informative articles by Alj Mary were included: "Computer 101: Some thoughts on PC's and software for the exhibitor" and "A designer looks at exhibiting." The first article discussed possible hardware and software choices for a prospective exhibitor. The second article was more philosophical and discussed how this new tool, the computer, will affect future exhibits.

A final article by Regis Hoffman, "The future of philatelic exhibiting," looked into the future and the advent of multimedia. Multimedia involves the merging of text, audio, and computer images and graphics into a single system. Stamp exhibits then need not be limited to static text and stamps. He suggested that future computer-generated paperless exhibits will allow the viewer to ask questions about the exhibit or give spoken commands, such as "Why is the cancel in red instead of black?" or "Show me the back of that cover."

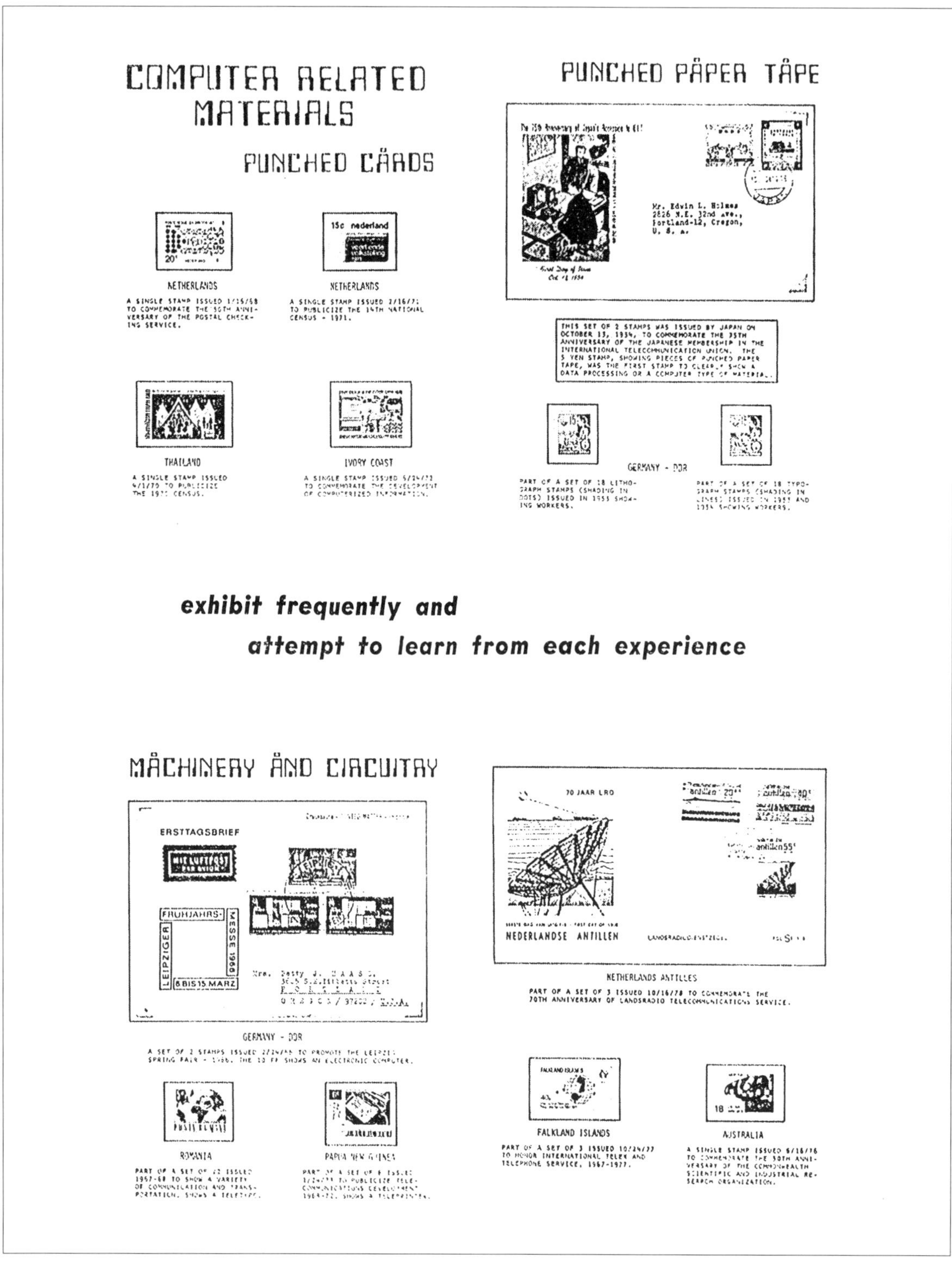

Figure 4.
A page from the final section of Donald Beuthal's exhibit "Computers on Stamps."

The Politics of War

FEATURING STAMPLESS COVERS TO A. H. STEPHENS
VICE PRESIDENT OF THE CONFEDERACY

The seeking of favors from those in high political office is not new. During the WAR BETWEEN THE STATES many people wrote to the Vice President of the Confederacy enlisting his aid for various reasons. Although most of the letters were destroyed, Mr. Stephens or his secretary would write an excerpt of the letters contents on the envelope. At times the notation was nothing more than the name of the sender; but often it was a request for help in procuring a military commission, a political appointment, or at times even money.

This one frame exhibit, in addition to featuring various stampless postal markings, also shows the diversity of requests received by Mr. Stephens.

Paid 5
Augusta, Georgia June 6, 1861 type I A

Baker & Caswell June 6, 1861 Augusta, Ga. Bills

The excerpts of the letters have been copied verbatim and are printed in *italics*.

Figure 5.
This page, from Conrad Bush's exhibit, "The Politics of War," was prepared using an IBM compatible 386SX computer.

Sample Album Pages

Todd Ronnei has created album pages on his Macintosh computer, which he has been using for the past six years. He started by using the MacDraw II program, which took some time to master, especially centering graphics and text within borders. He abandoned MacDraw when he found out how much easier WordPerfect could be.

Figure 6 is an example from his collection of Marshall Islands World War II stamps. Centering the stamp frame on the page is a snap: Select the graphic with the mouse and then choose Center. Ronnei uses 24-pound stock, acid-free Eaton Tecnaclear paper, designed especially for laser printers. His printer is a GCC PLP II, which features a straight paper-path option, so that heavier stock doesn't jam.

James Brinkley Jr. prepared album pages on a Macintosh LCII using the Aldus Pagemaker program. He prints the pages on 60-pound Vicksburg Vellum paper, which goes through his PLP II printer with no problems. Pagemaker is a versatile desktop-publishing program. Brinkley says it's easy to add any number of descriptive lines under each stamp. He can readily move text blocks and graphics anywhere on the page. Figure 7 is a sample page describing the grilled areas on the 1867 issues.

Robert Clough used Microsoft Word for Windows to create pages for his collection. He uses Linn Philatelic Product album pages, which are no longer produced. Clough uses the line-drawing capability of Microsoft Word 5.0 and various type fonts ranging from Helvetica 14 point for headers to 8 point for the stamp identification. Word includes a robust macro programming language to produce the various box sizes or page layouts desired. Figure 8 is a sample page for U.S. precancels from Union City, New Jersey. Note that this page contains spaces for 48 stamps. You really need a heavy stock to support this many stamps on one page.

L. Sue Weaver has used Print Shop Deluxe (PSD), a Windows graphics program from Broderbund Software, to create album pages. A sample sheet for the 1987 Red Cloud issue is shown in Figure 9. Weaver states that PSD is a very simple program to work in. Text and borders can be added anywhere in any dimensions and moved anywhere on the page or copied to another page. The width and styles of borders available are almost limitless. Centering and aligning are done by merely selecting the layout you want. The only drawback in designing pages with PSD is that there is no ruler, so all the border and frame dimensions are guesswork until Weaver gets one right to copy.

Robert Levy has been using an Amiga 2000 computer to create album pages. His Canadian collection used White Ace pages, so he continued with blank Canadian sheets, attempting to duplicate the White Ace format as closely as possible. Figure 10 shows a page of Newfoundland stamps.

The older versions of WordPerfect for DOS run on older and slower computers and give excellent results, especially if you have a good printer.

Figure 11 shows some of the possible box figures you can use to outline your stamps. Personally, I would not recommend the extra-thick line options. Special shadow effects are possible by using a thin line on two adjacent sides and a thicker line on the other two sides. The printed output has an attractive appearance, but you can't easily see the boxes on screen as you create them. Word Perfect 5.1 is text-oriented, so you do not normally see the boxes as you create them. You can get a graphics preview of your page by selecting the View Document choice from the print menu. This choice gives you a fair idea of what your printed page will look like.

You can also draw your boxes and see them on screen by using the line-draw ca-

50th ANNIVERSARY OF WORLD WAR II

Stamps of the Marshall Islands

First Combat By Flying Tigers, 1941
Issue Number 29

"On the morning of December 20, 1941, ten twin-engined Mitsubishi bombers, each loaded with incendiaries and 500-pound bombs, took off from the Japanese-held airfield at Hanoi and began a 300-mile flight to Kunming, the Chinese terminus of the Burma Road. The Japanese pilots anticipated a routine mission; they had been bombing Kunming every clear day for a year. But on this morning, approximately 30 miles southeast of Kunming, the pilots saw something unexpected--four fast fighter planes bearing down on them. The fighters, garish, fearsome-looking aircraft with their noses painted to resemble the toothy grins of giant sharks, raked past the Japanese formation with machine guns blazing. The attackers belonged to a colorful new American fighter group known as the Flying Tigers, and they had just flown their first combat mission in China."

--Don Moser, *China-Burma-India*

Figure 6.
A page from Todd Ronnei's collection of Marshall Islands World War II stamps.

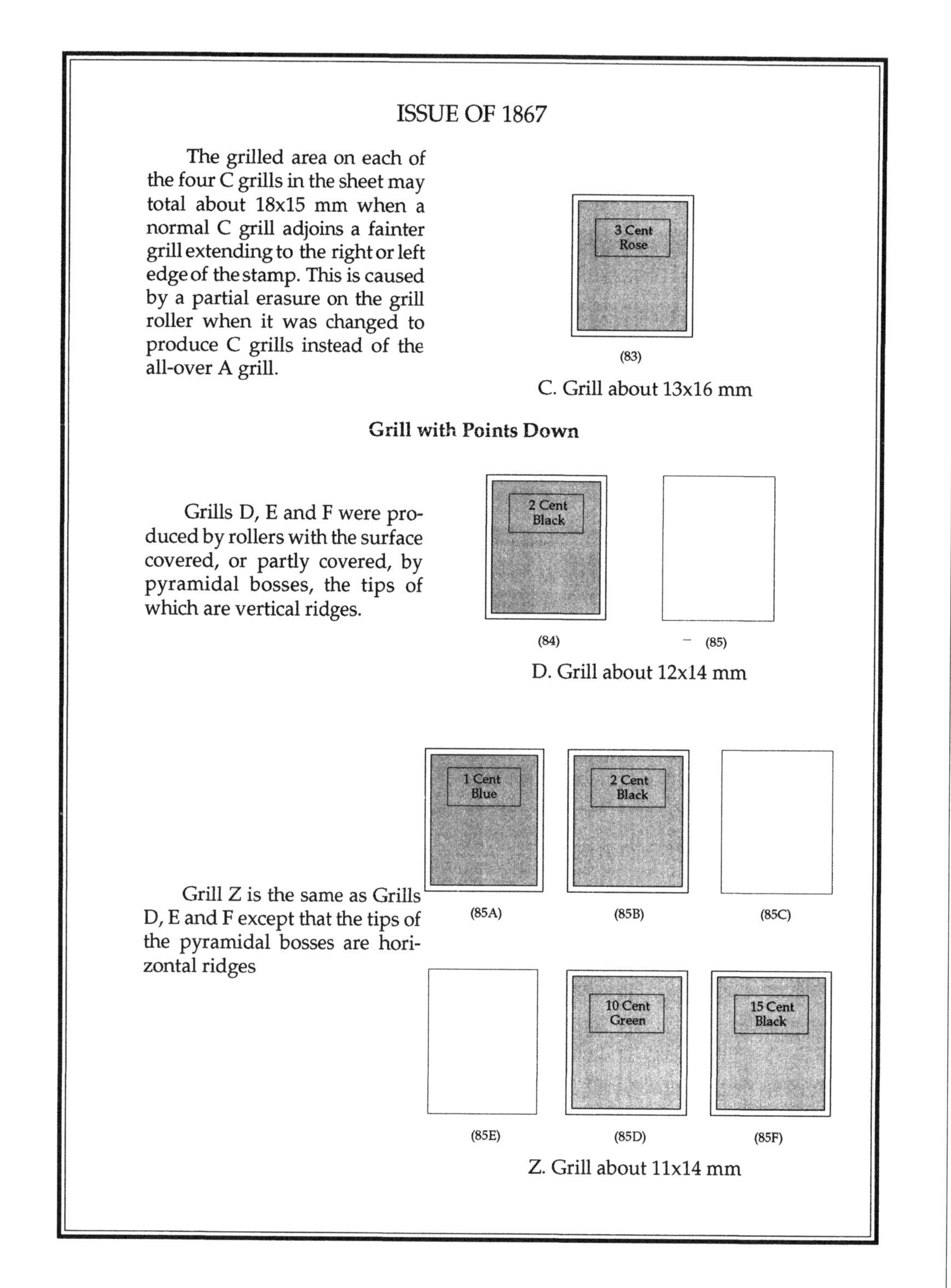

Figure 7.
A page from James Brinkley Jr.'s collection showing grilled areas on the 1867 issues.

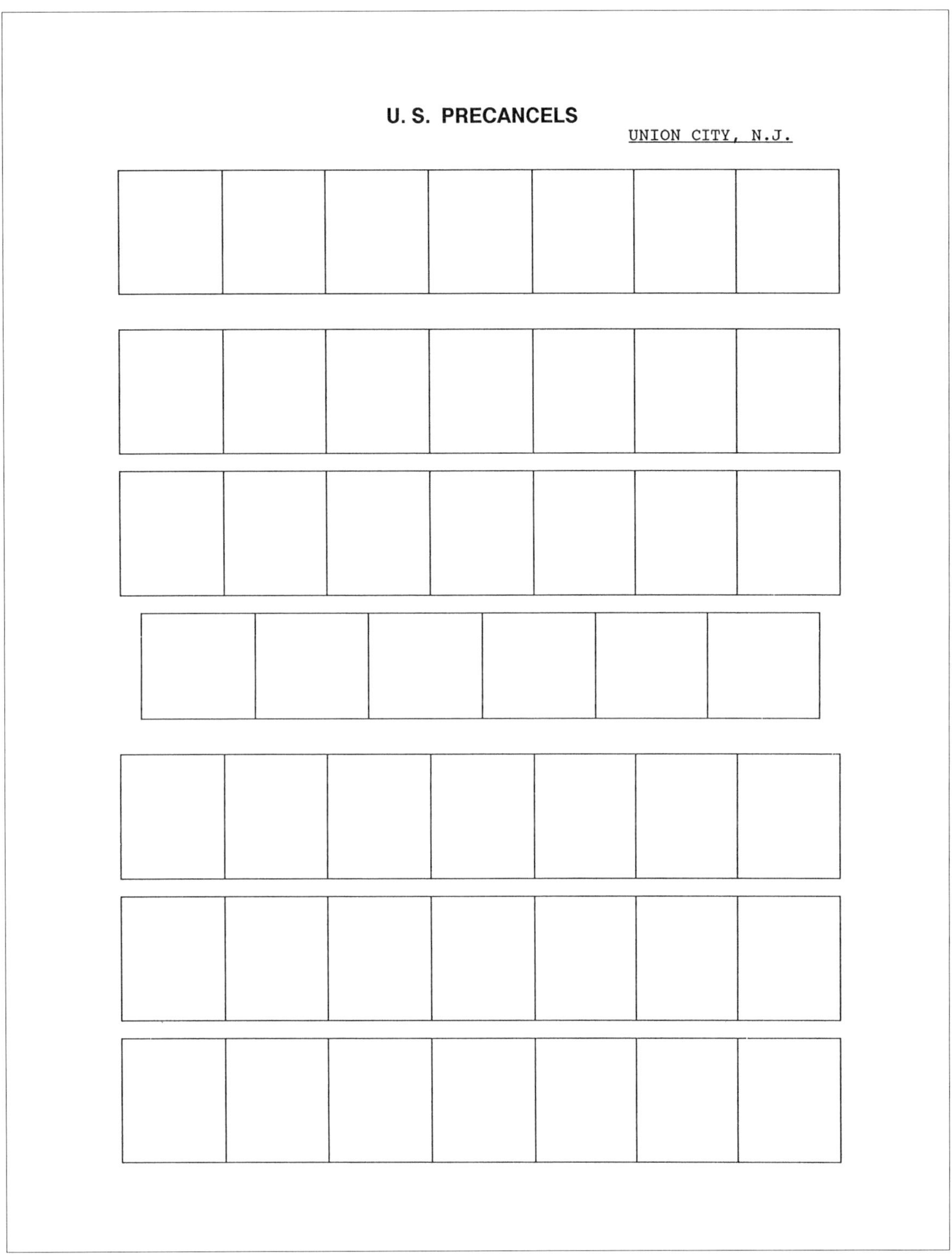

Figure 8.
U.S. precancels from Union City, New Jersey, are displayed on this page from Robert Clough's album. The page contains space for 48 stamps and requires heavy stock.

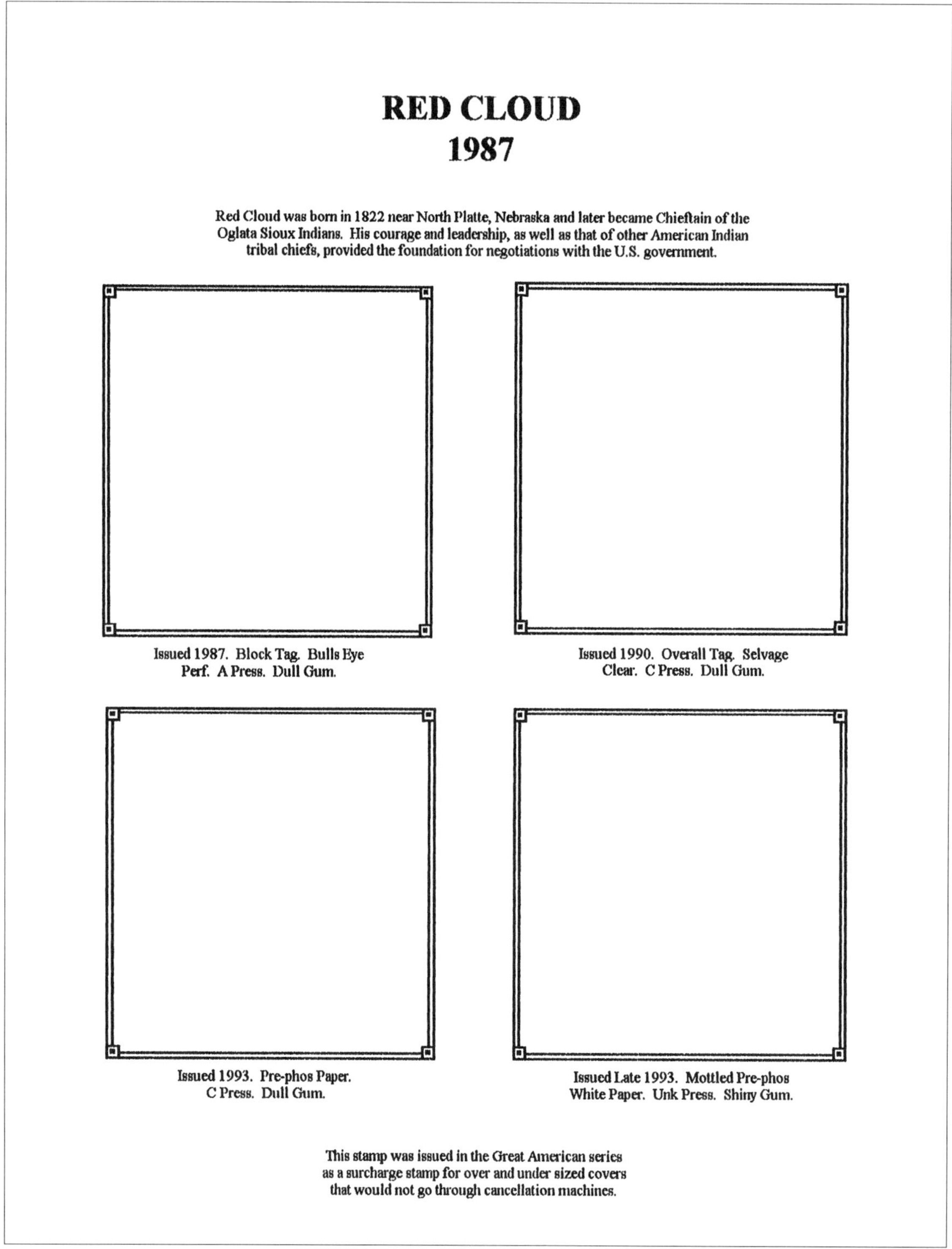

Figure 9.
A sample page from L. Sue Weaver's collection. She uses Print Shop Deluxe from Broderbund Software to create her album pages.

Figure 10.
Robert Levy attempts to duplicate the White Ace format with blank Canadian sheets.

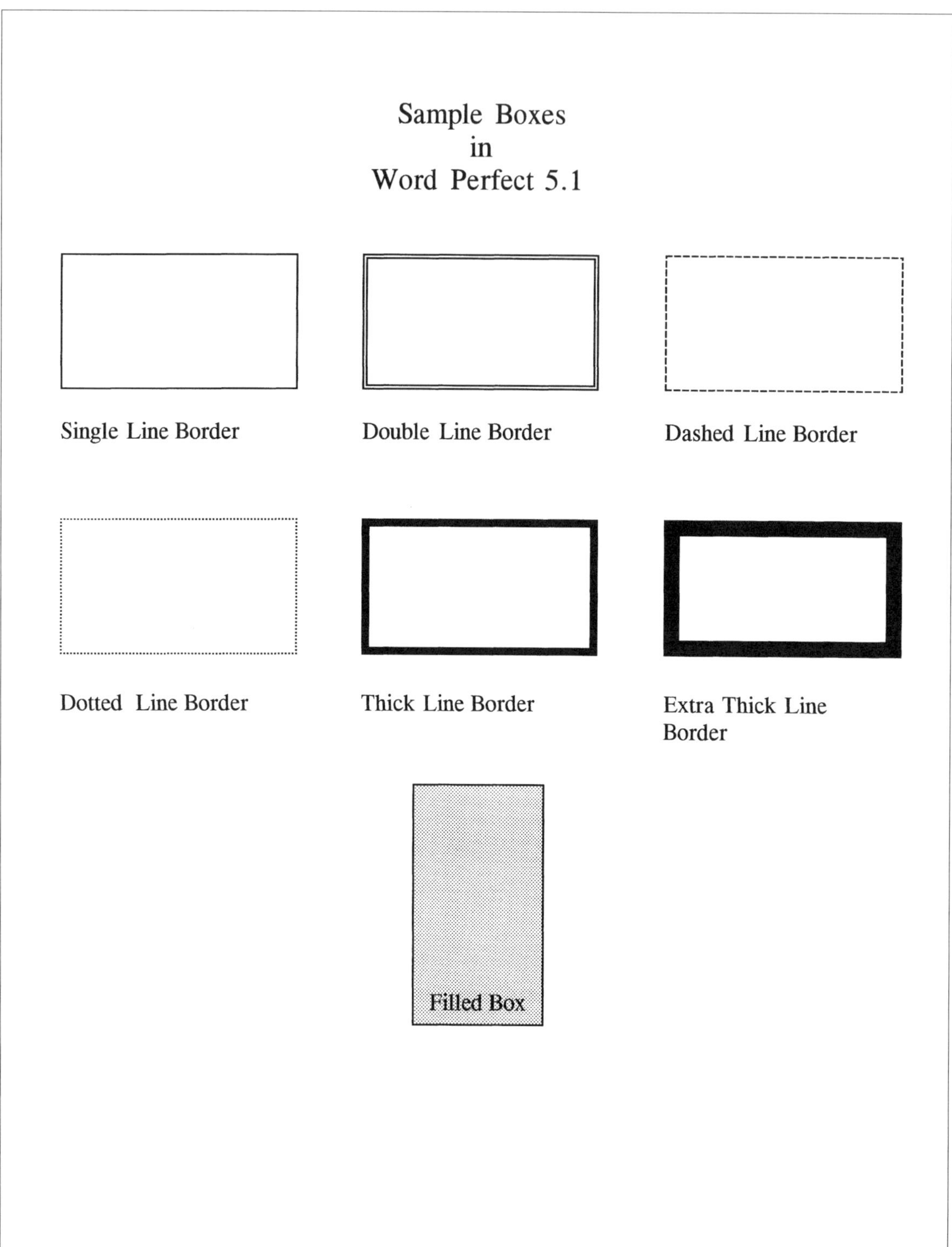

Figure 11.
Shown here are sample boxes that can be used to outline stamps.

pability of WordPerfect. You can't size your boxes as accurately as in the graphics mode, since the line drawing character takes up as much space as alphabetical characters. If you are working at the typical six lines per inch, the height of your box can only change in 0.167-inch steps. You also must use a mono-spaced font, i.e., one in which each character has the same width. Characters such as "W" and "M" take up more width than "i" or "j." You use the screen key (Control-F3) to select line-draw. You have an immediate choice of single or double lines or asterisks. If that's not sufficient, you can change the line-draw character to shaded blocks or any one specific character that you prefer. Once you've picked the type of line, you use the cursor keys to draw lines. You can erase lines by choosing Erase from the line-draw menu.

Many text-based word processors include box-drawing or framing capabilities. WordPerfect isn't the only one that does so, but it has been the largest-selling DOS word processor and implements the box creation feature quite well.

Normally you'd use Corel Print House for Windows 95 to create greeting cards, certificates, banners, signs and brochures. The program has limited drawing capabilities, but you can create rectangular boxes and specify their size and location to the nearest one-hundredth of an inch. You can choose from a number of line widths and characteristics, use a fill color within the boxes or create a shadow effect.

The program costs less than $30, so it's a low-cost means of creating album pages.

You can type text directly anywhere on the page, but you have more flexibility if you place the text inside a box. These text-box borders won't print. You can center the text in the box and move the box with its text around on the page as desired. The program includes more than 100 fonts, plus you can use any fonts that are already in-stalled in Windows. You can dress up your page design with a variety of clipart drawings, maps, flags and photographs. Figure 12 is obviously not a real album page, but it shows a sampling of the box (or mount) sizes and clips that can be provided. The program includes 5,000 clipart images and 1,000 full-color photos.

I started by picking a sign as my project, since the page size for a sign is 8½ by 11 inches. I used the rectangle tool from the Print House tool bar and placed a box on the page with an approximate location and size. I brought up a dialogue box for positioning the starting location of the first box at exactly 1 inch in from the left side and 1 inch down from the top of the paper. Another dialogue box lets you specify the exact size of the box. I had to make a few calculations to specify the starting locations, i.e., top-left corner, of additional boxes so I could get them reasonably spaced on the page.

Once I created one box, it was easy to duplicate the same size box and place it in other locations on the page. You'll need to do a bit more work if your stamps aren't all the same size.

You have two choices when installing Print House. A full installation will copy most program files to your hard disk and requires about 16 megabytes of space. A limited installation puts a minimal number of files on your hard disk, only using 2 megabytes. Most program files remain on the CD-ROM, so the program runs somewhat slower with this method. In both cases you need to have the CD-ROM disk in your drive to run the program.

The user manual includes 18 pages of instructions on using the program and several hundred pages of illustrations in full color of all the graphic files that are included on the CD-ROM. You can also import graphic images from other formats.

Be aware that the file size of your album page can become very large if you include a lot of graphics on your sheet. You probably wouldn't put a map, a flag and a picture of the Sydney Opera House all on one page, but the file for Figure 12 took up 1.2 megabytes of hard-disk space. Removing the map and picture resulted in a file size of 21 kilobytes, a reduction of 98 percent!

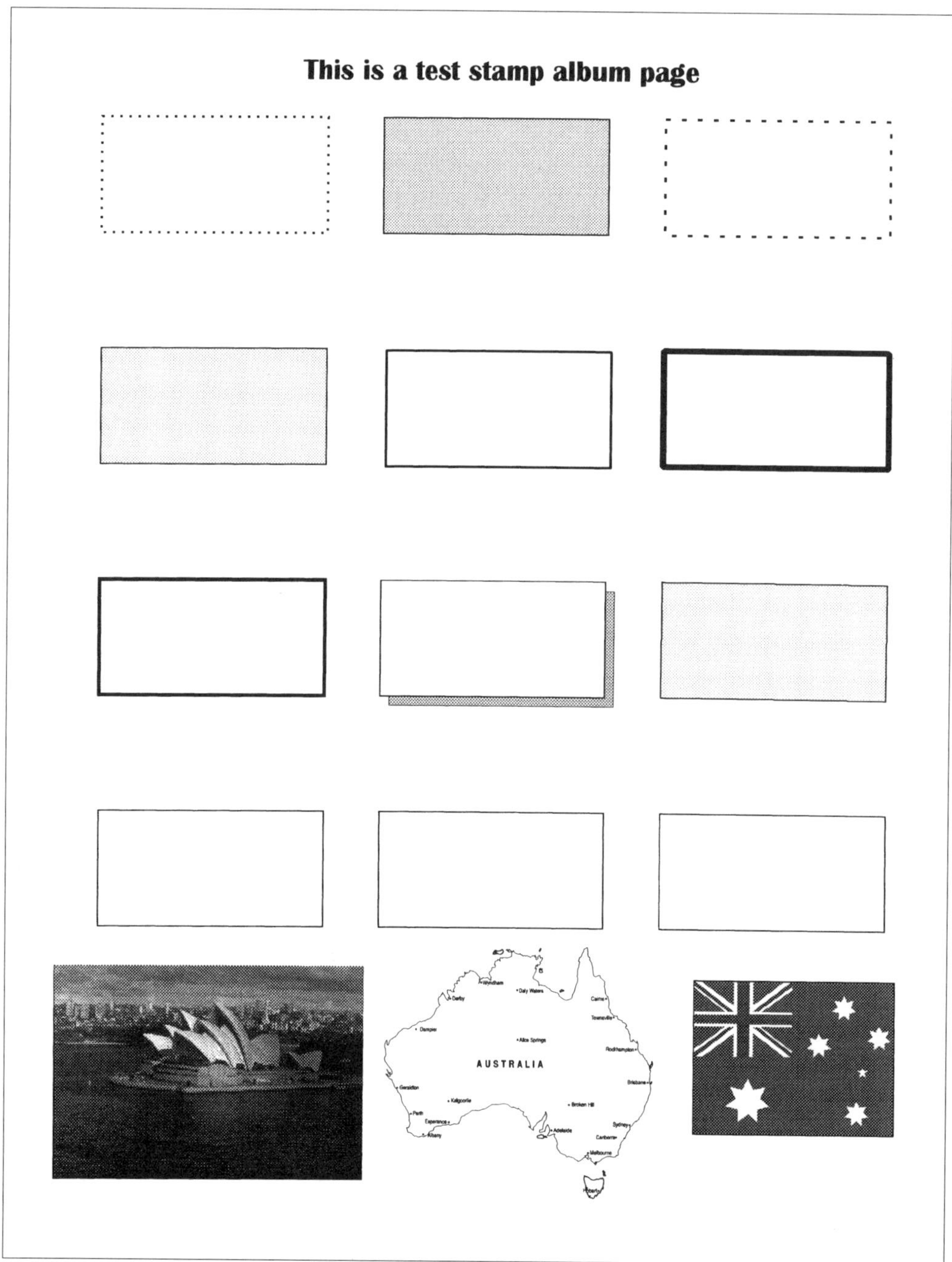

Figure 12.
A mock-up of an album page showing a sampling of the box sizes and clipart that can be obtained using Print House.

Album Pages Using Spreadsheets

Windows spreadsheet programs are readily adapted to designing album pages. Quattro Pro is especially suitable for this purpose, since you can specify the exact height and width of each spreadsheet cell, in either inches or centimeters. You place a border around all the edges of the cell that acts as a frame for your mounted stamp. You can place information, such as a catalog number, within the frame. You can also use the cells above and below your frame to provide descriptive information about your stamp.

Quattro Pro allows you to import images, so you can insert a scanned image of a stamp inside the frame if you so desire. You can use different fonts, font sizes and font effects, such as boldface, underline and italics in your text. In fact, all the common formatting effects, such as center, right or left justification are available. The row and column gridlines display on screen for guidance as you set up the page, but only the border effects and text show up on paper when you print a page.

You can put a border around the whole page, if desired. You'll still need to calculate the distance between the framed cells in order to achieve the proper spacing on your page. Once you have created a frame of the desired size, you can record a macro command that can be played back automatically to create additional frames of the same size. You can also save entire pages with frames without text and copy them to other pages that you want to create with the same or similar format.

Quattro Pro is a true three-dimensional spreadsheet, consisting of the usual rows and columns as well as pages. Each page is identified by a report tab at the bottom of the screen display. You can have a total of 255 pages in one "notebook," as Corel, the current program supplier, refers to the overall file. You could design one page to display four stamps, then easily copy the format to other pages. You would then modify the headings and descriptions of the stamps as needed.

I spent about an hour setting up the illustrated Australian stamp page (Figure 13). This was my initial effort with this program, although I have used other spreadsheet programs in the past. Additional pages could be created more quickly, especially if the stamp arrangement is identical to an already-designed page. The length of the stamp descriptions and background information could be reduced, if desired. The second illustration (Figure 14) shows the page as it appears on screen with the row and column gridlines shown.

Other graphical spreadsheet programs include similar capabilities, but they will require you to size the row height using point size ($1/72$ of an inch) and column width using character count. You may have to do some draft printing with various values to determine the desired cell size.

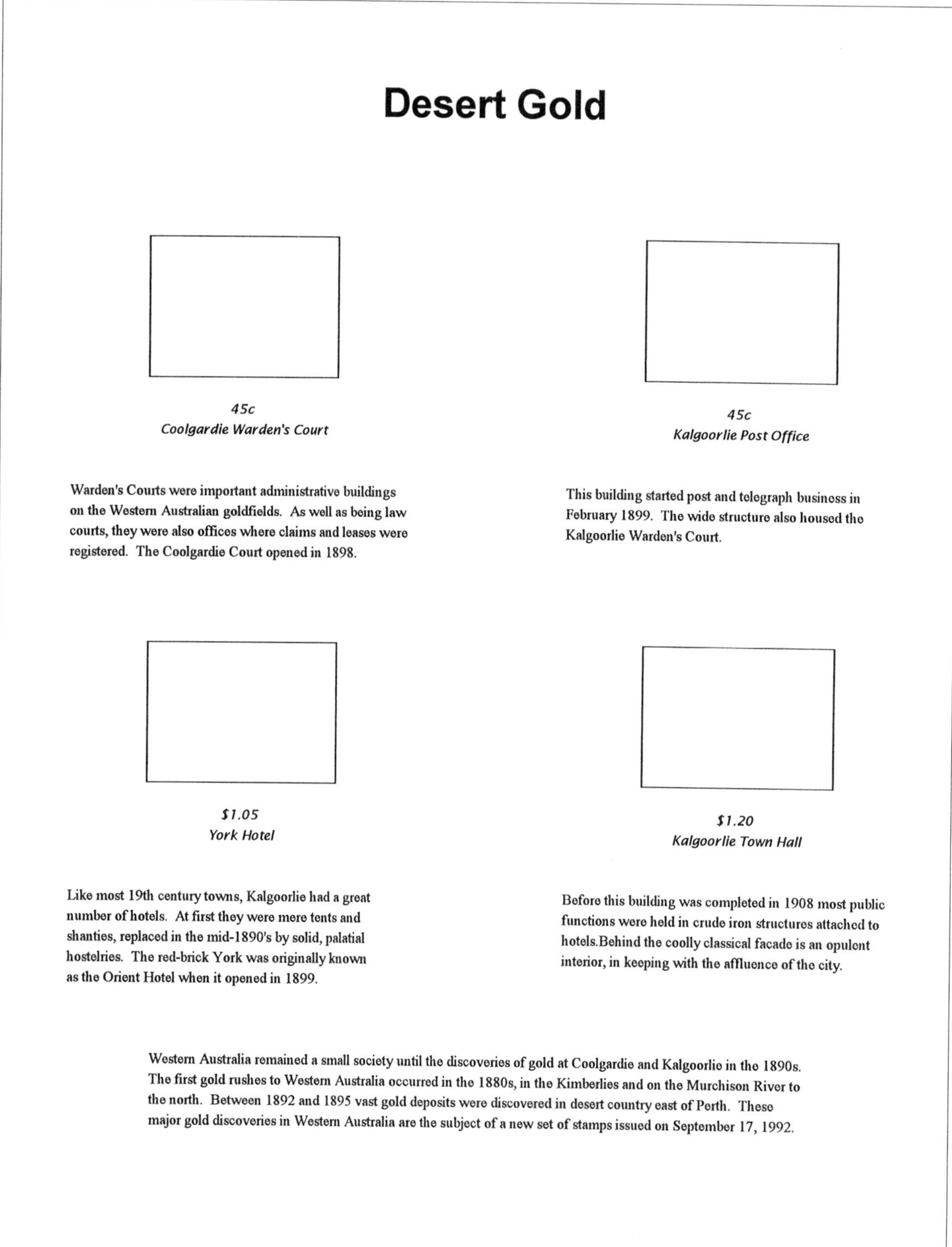

Figure 13.
This page for Australian stamps was designed using Quattro Pro, a spreadsheet program. Figure 14 shows how the page appears on screen.

Desert Gold

A	A	B	C	D	E	F	G
1							
2							
3							
4							
5							
6		*45c*				*45c*	
7		*Coolgardie Warden's Court*				*Kalgoorlie Post Office*	
8							
9							
10		Warden's Courts were important administrative buildings			This building started post and telegraph business in		
11		on the Western Australian goldfields. As well as being law			February 1899. The wide structure also housed the		
12		courts, they were also offices where claims and leases were			Kalgoorlie Warden's Court.		
13		registered. The Coolgardie Court opened in 1898.					
14							
15							
16							
17							
18							
19							
20		*$1.05*				*$1.20*	
21		*York Hotel*				*Kalgoorlie Town Hall*	
22							
23							
24		Like most 19th century towns, Kalgoorlie had a great			Before this building was completed in 1908 most public		
25		number of hotels. At first they were mere tents and			functions were held in crude iron structures attached to		
26		shanties, replaced in the mid-1890's by solid, palatial			hotels.Behind the coolly classical facade is an opulent		
27		hostelries. The red-brick York was originally known			interior, in keeping with the affluence of the city.		
28		as the Orient Hotel when it opened in 1899.					
29							
30							
31							
32		Western Australia remained a small society until the discoveries of gold at Coolgardie and Kalgoorlie in the 1890s.					
33		The first gold rushes to Western Australia occurred in the 1880s, in the Kimberlies and on the Murchison River to					
34		the north. Between 1892 and 1895 vast gold deposits were discovered in desert country east of Perth. These					
35		major gold discoveries in Western Australia are the subject of a new set of stamps issued on September 17, 1992.					
36							
37							
38							
39							
40							

Figure 14.
This shows how the album page in Figure 13 looks as a spreadsheet on screen.

Dedicated Album-Page Programs

Three Windows programs for creating album or exhibit pages have been released. I have not located any Macintosh programs specifically designed for page creation. One Mac user states that it's so easy to use the commercial Mac desktop publishing programs that there's no need for such a program!

Album Pro is by far the easiest and most versatile dedicated program to use. Stamp Album Page Designer works well but has limitations, not the least of which is an aversion to identity. The program supplier provides only a mailing address, which is a commercial postal drop location. Letters from Integrity Software and Computing are not signed, and there's no phone number or e-mail address listed. My Album, the most recent dedicated program, connects album pages with an inventory listing, a novel feature. There are too many unresolved problems in creating pages to recommend purchase of this program. My Album does not include a manual, another major drawback.

Album Pro

Jim Fowler and Walter Ezell, both stamp collectors, developed this program initially for their own use. They wanted to design album and exhibit pages on a computer and were unhappy with the deficiencies of existing software.

The most unusual feature of Album Pro is the use of a database to aid in designing the pages. The database of U.S. stamps issued through November 1995 contains all the information about each stamp that you need to display on your album page. The database knows the height and width of each stamp and includes the words needed for a caption and heading. Once you select the stamp, Album Pro puts the properly sized boxes on the page with the appropriate text above and below the boxes. The software calculates the size of each box, and aligns and spaces them automatically.

The manual states that you can create an album page in less than five minutes. The first page I created took longer than that, but once you've got the hang of entering the stamp information on a grid format, the entry speed increases. Figure 15 shows the page I created for the National Parks issue of 1934. I used the stamp descriptions stored in the database as is, although you can delete, change or embellish the headings and captions for each stamp. Figure 16 shows the entry screen for the program. You can't see the entire page at once on the entry screen, but you can scroll up and down the page or call up a full-screen print preview to see what your page will look like before printing it out.

Album Pro ships with a set of four tutorials that provides an easy path to learn the program. These guides step the user through simple page creation followed by more complex designs. You can specify multiple frame sizes to handle strips or blocks of multiple stamps from menu choices on screen. You can also create generic entries for different stamp sizes from other countries. Album Pro even provides for triangular or diamond-shaped frames, if desired.

According to the manual, Album Pro supports page sizes up to 12 by 12 inches. Of course, you'll need a printer that will handle a larger-than-normal page size.

What's wrong with the program? First, there's no on-screen help provided. Most Windows programs provide a context-sensitive help system that provides information on how to use the program. You've got to rely on the manual with Album Pro. Fortunately, the manual is well-written, nicely illustrated, and includes a table of contents

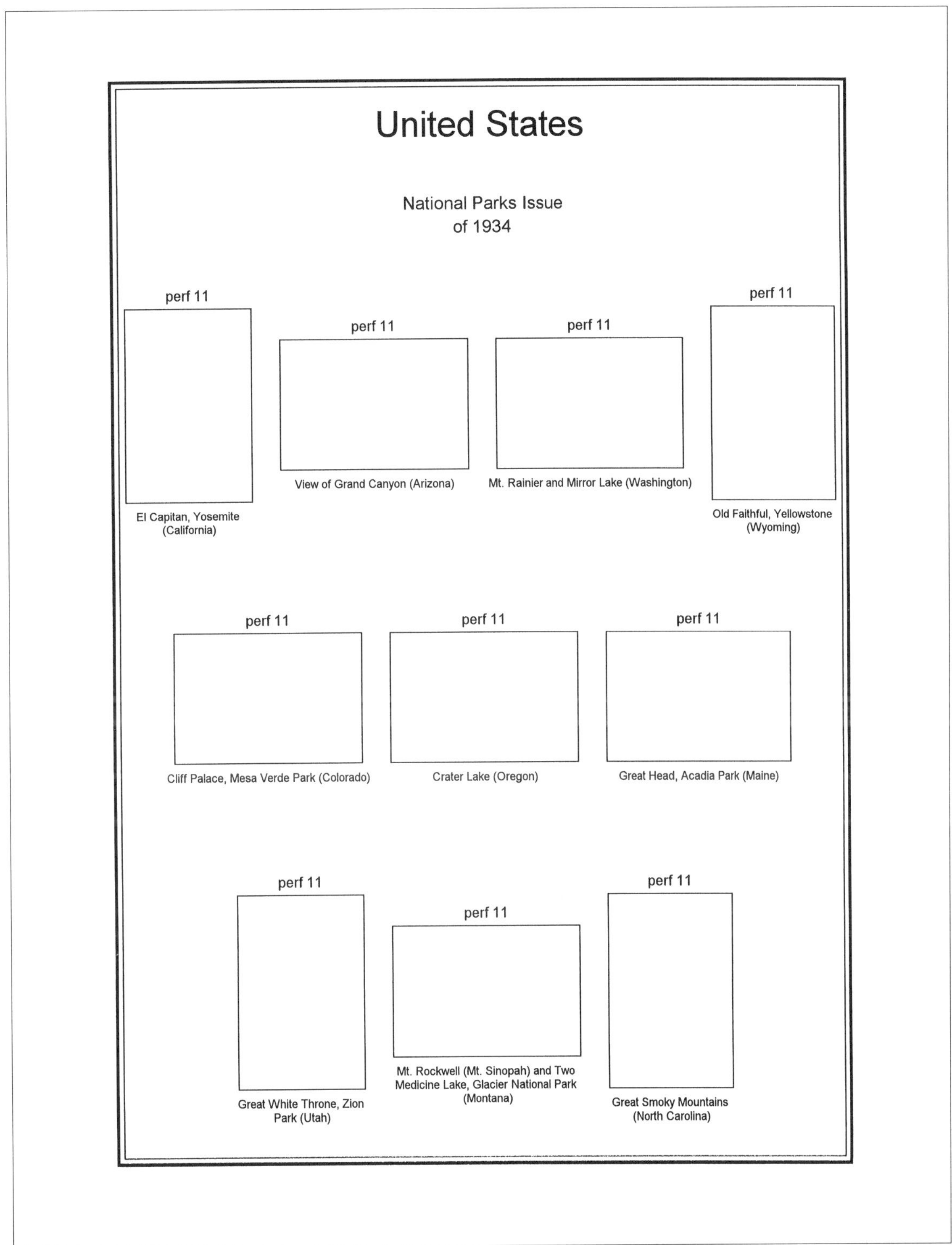

Figure 15.
A page created for the U.S. National Parks issue using Album Pro.

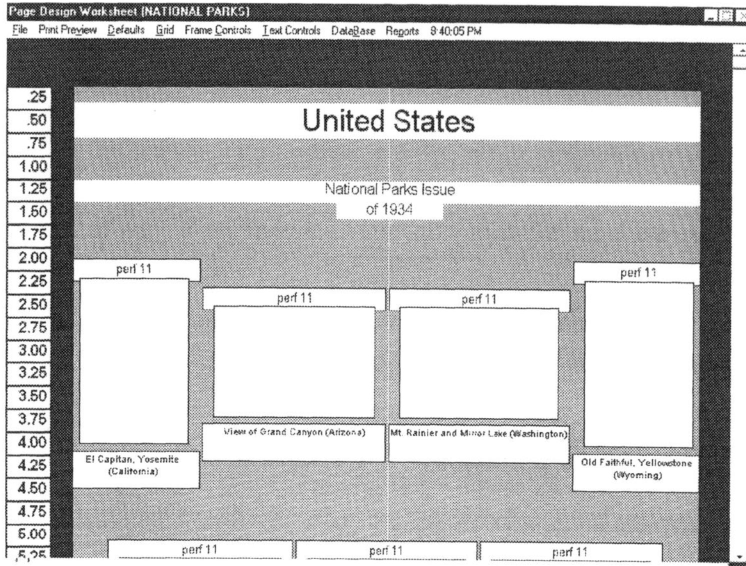

Figure 16.
The entry screen for the program used to create the page shown in Figure 15.

and thorough index.

The second shortcoming is that the database used by the program doesn't include Scott catalog numbers. The authors mention this deficiency in the manual, attributing the problem to their inability to license numbers from catalog publishers for their "proprietary lists." Album Pro includes its own listing of stamp numbers. You can print out the database listing and coordinate these numbers with Scott yourself; in fact, you can even add the Scott (or any other catalog system) number to the database record for that stamp. However, you must use Album Pro's ID number when you call up stamp information to create a frame on your page. Album Pro's ID numbers for the National Parks issue are 07270 through 07360 (numbers run by tens, not by units). Corresponding Scott numbers are 740 through 749.

You can't place graphic images, such as a country flag or map, on your album page with Album Pro. If you want this capability, you can leave a blank space on your album page. Then run the page through the printer twice, once for the stamp frames and once for the graphic image, using another program.

Album Pro's database uses a Microsoft Access format. Since I have a copy of this database program, I found it helpful to run the Access program at the same time I was running Album Pro. By switching between the two programs, I was able to find the proper Album Pro ID numbers by searching for "National Parks" in the Access database and then entering these numbers in the page-design program. Album Pro won't let you change the ID numbers in the database within the program, but you can change the numbers in Access, if desired.

Album Pro is designed for IBM-compatible computers running Windows 3.1 or later versions. You need a 386 or better processor with 4 megabytes of RAM and up to 10 megabytes of hard-disk space. My Album Pro directory contains only 4 megabytes of files. The space requirements will grow slowly as you add your design work to the Save Page file and as new yearly supplements are applied to the database.

The company offers a refund, except for shipping charges, if you are not satisfied with the program within 30 days.

The Well-Centered Publishing Company
P.O. Box 8459
Greenville, SC 29604
$59.95 plus $4 shipping
Phone: (803) 235-5019
Fax: (803) 235-1350
Orders: (800) 648-5517
e-mail: albumpro@aol.com

Stamp Album Page Designer

Stamp Album Page Designer (SAPD) provides a simple graphical means to easily design album or exhibit pages. I have included a sample album page (see Figure 17) that you would not likely design yourself. I modified the frames for each stamp to show the variety of borders that can be provided. Essentially you can use any combination of single-, double- or triple-line borders with three possible thicknesses for the lines. The individual stamp borders, whether single, double or triple, all have the same outside dimensions. Note that the area allowed for the stamp within the border differs for each of these arrangements.

The program comes with a concise, well-written 24-page manual that first explains some terminology (page, border, header block, page number block), then lists the various menu commands that are available as you create a page. As you can see in Figure 18, a toolbar is provided as an alternative to the top row menus for most of the major commands. The manual includes a table of contents but no index. An index really isn't necessary.

Useful hints are listed in the back of the manual. The author recommends using the heaviest paper your printer can handle for the most satisfactory results. If your printer will not accommodate heavy paper, he suggests using a card-stock base with your album page glued to the card stock.

The Express Layout tool allows you to create an entire page of stamp frames with a single command action. The frames don't have any titles and must all be the same size and style, but you can edit each one to give it the unique characteristics required.

The program will automatically position the frames on the page so they are centered vertically and horizontally. You'll get an error message if you try to put more frames on a page than there's room for. You can align stamp frames of differing sizes in one row either by the top or bottom of the frame or have them centered on the line.

Each stamp frame has a top title, bottom title and tag available. You'd typically use the tag, which appears in the middle of the frame, to identify the catalog number of a stamp. You can leave any of these titles blank, if desired. You can select any Windows font, size and type (normal, bold, italic or underlined) for each stamp title.

I have minor complaints about SAPD. I was not able to create a description longer than one line for each stamp. I often like to include some detailed information about the subject shown on a stamp, but I couldn't do that here. As far as I can tell, you can only specify the dimensions of each stamp frame in inches. An option to use metric measurements would be helpful.

The program is ideal, though, for designing pages for a great variety of stamps when only minimal descriptions are required. I also have some reservations concerning support; no phone numbers or e-mail addresses are provided. Mail communications were answered eventually, but Integrity apparently wants to be known as an anonymous company. Nobody signs their letters, even for a reviewer!

Integrity Software and Computing
23052-H Alicia Parkway #414
Mission Viejo, California 92692
$60 postpaid
No phone, fax or e-mail address

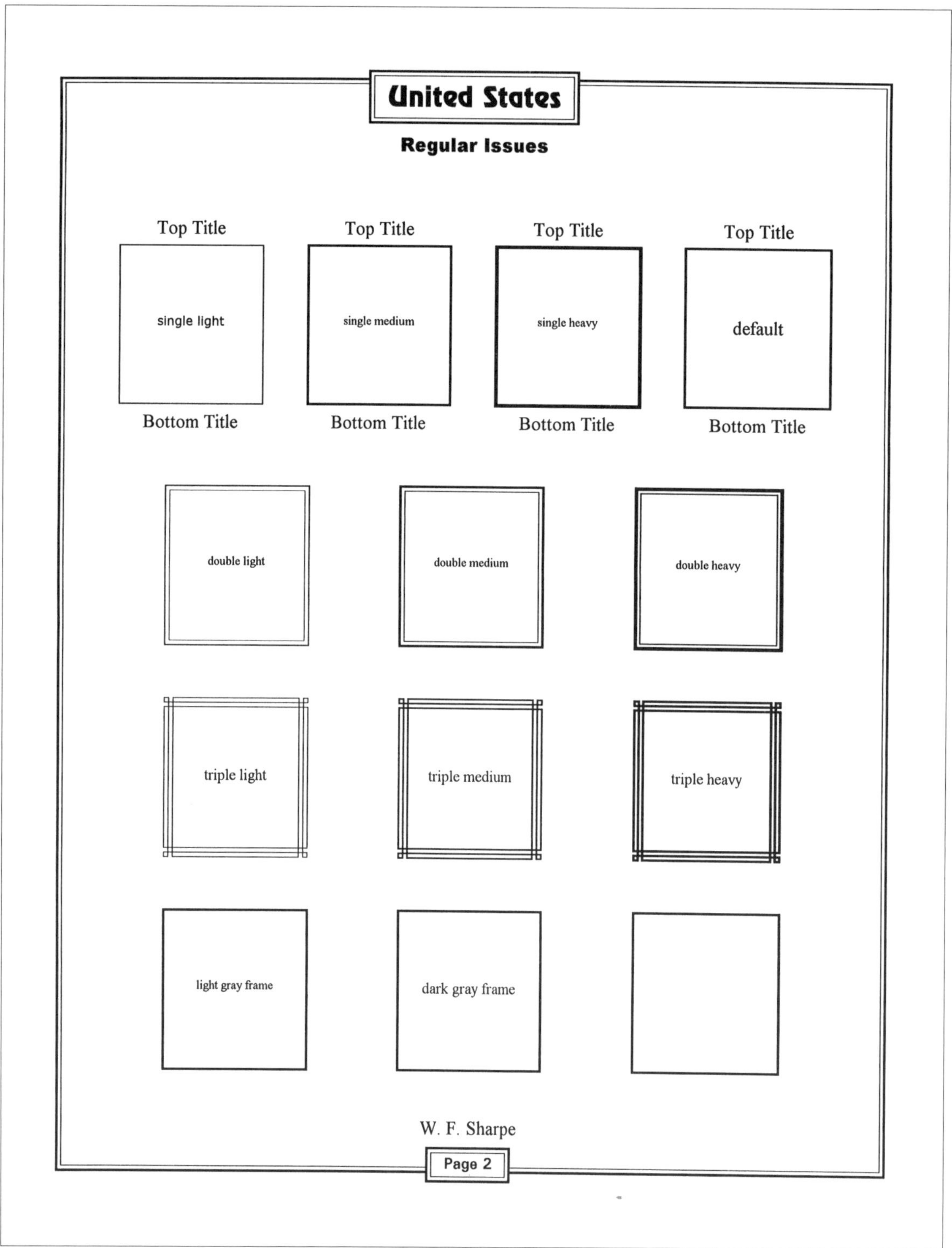

Figure 17.
A sample album page created using Stamp Album Page Designer. This shows the variety of borders that can be produced.

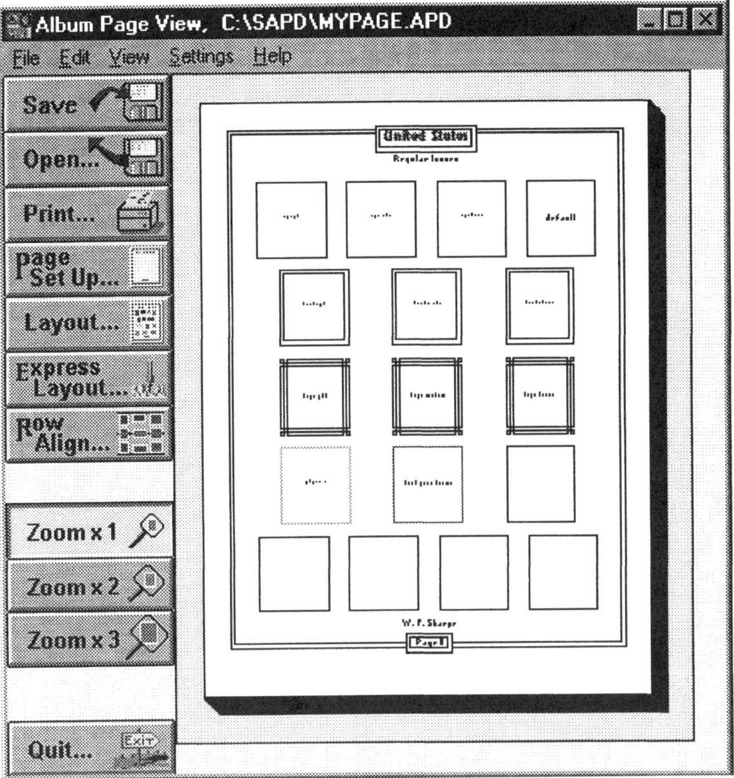

Figure 18.
The entry screen for Stamp Album Page Designer,
showing the toolbar on the left.

My Album

My Album from Drummond House of America, advertised as a combination inventory and album-page design program, has had a checkered history since its initial appearance in the latter part of 1995.

The first review copy I received, priced at $160, was virtually unusable. There was no manual, the help system was indecipherable and the sample printouts of album pages were visually disappointing.

Two price reductions have brought the price to a much more reasonable $49.95 for the current version 1.2. There's still no manual, but the help system includes a tutorial, which can be printed, that explains how to set up both portions of the program. More sample pages are included, but most of them are still problematic.

Computer-program prices have been coming down in recent years; software manufactures have been reducing the size of the manuals included with the programs as a means of keeping their costs down. Still, commercial programs generally include a manual that tells the user how to install the program and gives at least a summary of how the program operates.

I expect to use my printer and my paper to print out manuals for shareware and freeware programs, but when I buy a program by paying in advance, I want some printed guidance on how to proceed. My Album ships in a small plastic disk holder that includes a small (3½-inch square) sheet telling me how to view or print the tutorial before loading the program. That approach is insufficient.

There are a few typographical errors in the tutorial, and it would help if some illustrations were added. In general, though, you can learn how to use the program by following the instructions.

The inventory section lets you create records for your collection. You create one or more major category listings based on country or theme. You can divide these lists into subcategories, such as airmails, revenue or want list. You can select a catalog of your choice, since you will be entering catalog numbers yourself. The program does not include a database of stamp records to help you begin.

Once you've performed these steps, you can enter information about individual stamps. The only required entry is catalog number. Optional entries are catalog price, purchase price, condition, type (plate block, single, sheet, line pair, and so on) and notes. The program will automatically sort your list based on catalog number.

The catalog number is an alphanumeric field, since catalog numbers often include leading and trailing letters in addition to the number. Humans know that the proper order for airmail stamps should be C1, C2, C3, C10, C11, C100. An alphanumeric sort by the computer would give this order: C1, C10, C100, C11, C2, C3. The computer can only follow the rules programmers provide for it to use. You need to add leading zeros to this field for proper sorting. Your catalog numbers should look like this for proper sorting: C001, C002, C003, C010, C011, C100.

Figure 19 shows an inventory listing of some Canadian stamps.

You can obtain a listing of your inventory, either complete or with selected stamps, displayed on screen or printed out. Only one report format is available.

I suspect most prospective buyers are interested in the album-page portion of the program rather than the database. Setting up a page requires a few preliminary steps using the Options/Preferences menu. A drawing grid, a series of dots that don't print, helps you align your work and can be set with distances between dots as desired. You can use either metric or English measurements. You'll want to set the page size to letter and orientation to portrait.

Various drawing tools are provided.

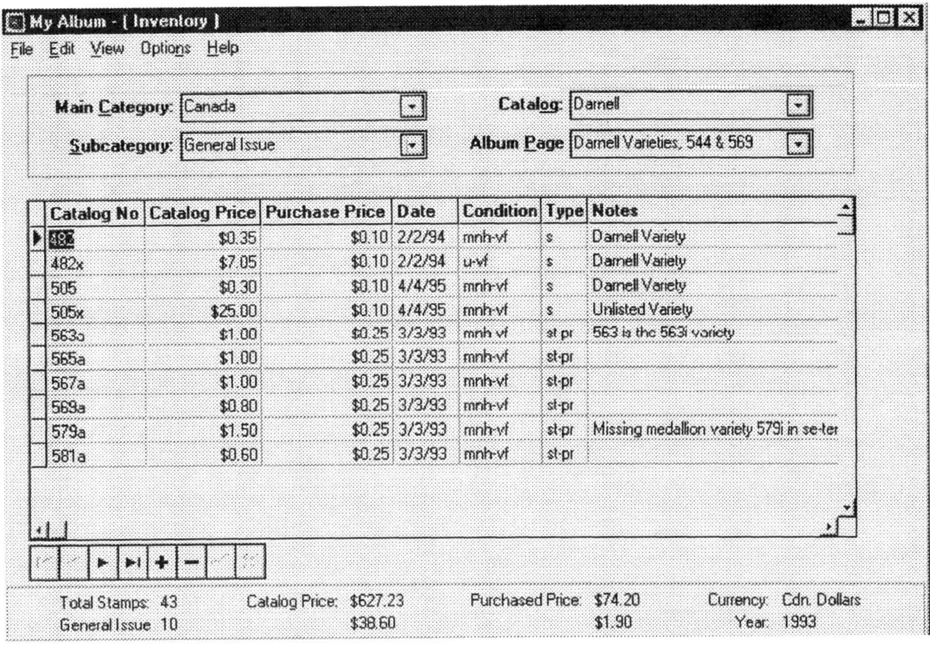

Catalog No	Catalog Price	Purchase Price	Date	Condition	Type	Notes
482	$0.35	$0.10	2/2/94	mnh-vf	s	Darnell Variety
482x	$7.05	$0.10	2/2/94	u-vf	s	Darnell Variety
505	$0.30	$0.10	4/4/95	mnh-vf	s	Darnell Variety
505x	$25.00	$0.10	4/4/95	mnh-vf	s	Unlisted Variety
563a	$1.00	$0.25	3/3/93	mnh-vf	st-pr	563 is the 563i variety
565a	$1.00	$0.25	3/3/93	mnh-vf	st-pr	
567a	$1.00	$0.25	3/3/93	mnh-vf	st-pr	
569a	$0.80	$0.25	3/3/93	mnh-vf	st-pr	
579a	$1.50	$0.25	3/3/93	mnh-vf	st-pr	Missing medallion variety 579i in se-ter
581a	$0.60	$0.25	3/3/93	mnh-vf	st-pr	

Figure 19.
An inventory listing of Canadian stamps created using My Album.

You use the rectangular tool for creating your page borders and stamp-mount frames. You can resize a shape after you've drawn it, move it or make copies. It's fairly straightforward to create a page with most stamps the same size, once you have decided on the size of one or two stamps. A text tool is available for adding titles and descriptions on your page.

By default, the program puts a border around your text. The tutorial tells you how to remove the border. I think most users prefer text without borders; it might have been a wiser choice to have the program put text on the page without borders and have the user make a change if a border is desired.

Figure 20 is one of the sample album pages included with the program. I modified it to remove the border around the title text box.

This program still has bugs in it. When I tried to edit the text box on one sample album page and clicked the OK button af-ter I finished changing it, the text box disappeared. I used Edit/Undelete to bring the text box back, but that's not the way the program should work. Also, when you try to edit text, the text is reset to whatever the default font and size are, rather than the text that you originally set up.

My Album includes a stamp-link feature so you can switch from the inventory record of a stamp to the album page that displays that stamp.

My Album has been improved from its initial release. The reduced price is a plus, but problems still remain.

Drummond House of America
212 Raymond Road, Unit 3
Nottingham, NH 03290
$60
Phone: (800) 649-8824
Web address:
http://www.myalbum.com/myalbum.htm

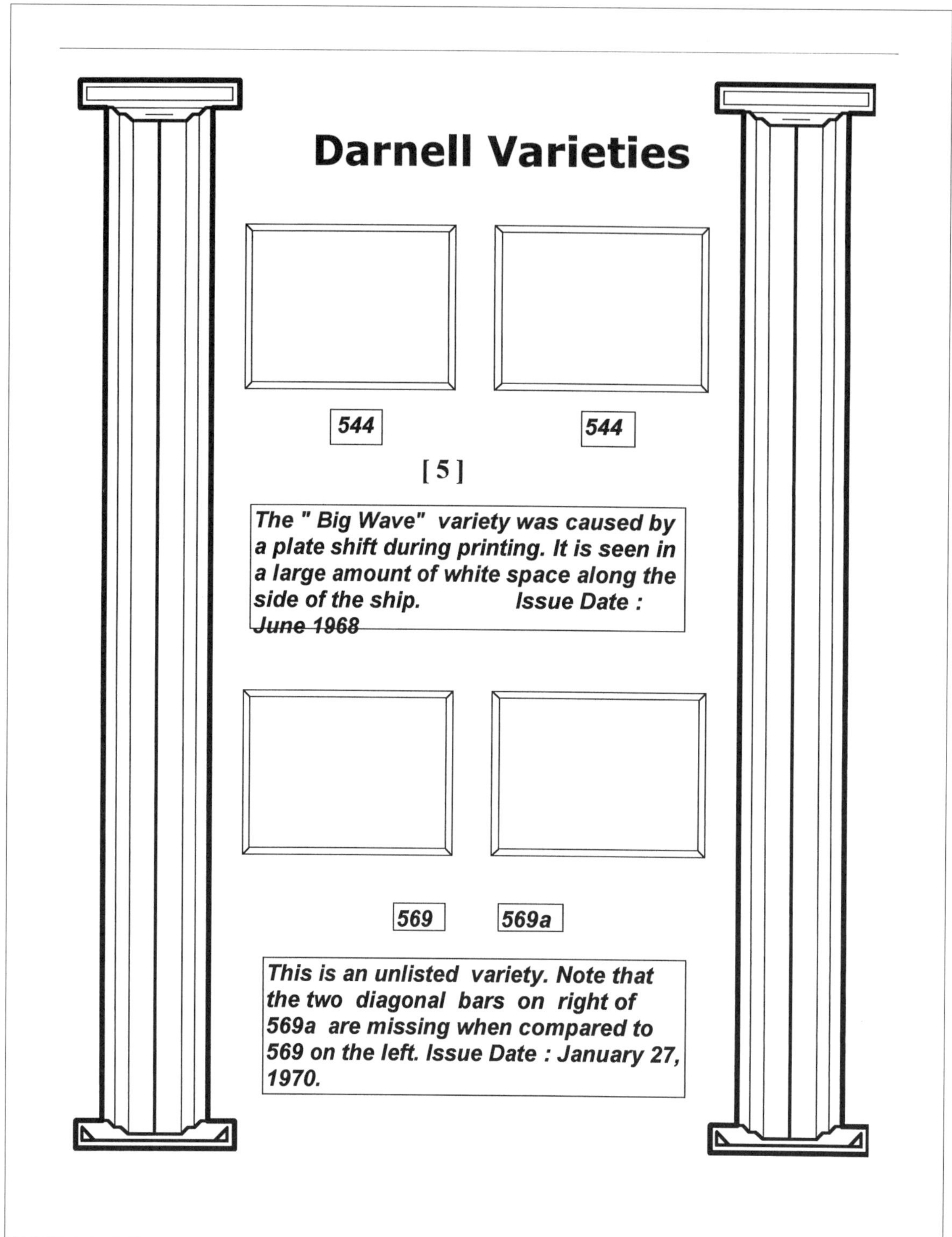

Figure 20.
A sample album page from My Album. The borders around the text can be removed.

Chapter 6

CD-ROMs

More Stamp Images than You'll Ever Need

CD-ROMs are a natural medium for stamp images. Graphics files take up a lot of disk space. Current CD-ROM technology allows up to 650 megabytes of readily accessible data storage on a 4.75-inch diameter disk. Even though stamp images are small, numerous stamps have been issued. Without the use of CD-ROMs, providing images for one country's issues would soon exhaust many owner's hard-disk capacity.

These disks look just like their audio counterparts even to the jewel-case packaging, but they are designed for use in a CD-ROM player in a personal computer.

CD-ROMs for stamp collectors come in several varieties. Some are electronic versions of stamp catalogs, some are strictly pictorial and some provide inventory features. EZ Stamps is primarily a database program, although the stamp images associated with the program are provided on CD-ROM. Look for a discussion of this program in the chapter on inventory programs.

Most of the disks mentioned in this chapter were released in the last two years. Expect to see many additional releases in the near future.

Additional CD-ROMs have been or will be published in addition to the ones mentioned below. These include PhilaRom for Windows, covering Dutch stamps; Russian Stampomania; Sassone's Italian catalog; and a possible Michel catalog.

Encyclodedia of U.S. Postage Stamps

The first release of *Encyclopedia of U.S. Postage Stamps* features scanned color images of 2,400 U.S. stamps with historical background information provided for each stamp. The third edition, released in 1996, includes more than 2,750 face-different stamps, including all stamps issued in 1995.

Unlike many CDs, you don't have to install any special software on your hard disk to start the program. The program will run from Windows or a DOS prompt if you are using an IBM-compatible computer. Clicking on the PowerCD icon starts the program if you are using a Macintosh computer. Figure 21 shows the main screen.

The press release describes the program as multimedia, which is technically true. There's some background music at the start, and you can listen to a narrator speak the words that appear on the screen in several of the presentations. You also hear a brief voice description for each stamp image as you view it.

There were no Scott catalog numbers or values associated with the stamps in the first release, but Minkus numbers have been added beginning with the second edition. There are several indexes available to help locate a stamp image. You can probably locate a stamp fairly quickly by its year of issue.

The disk includes a word-search feature, which looks for the appearance of any word you type in a dialogue box. The search is quite fast, considering the amount of information stored on the disk, but you can only search on one word at a time. I tried to find "Francis Scott Key" without success. Looking for "Key" resulted in 97 "hits," only a couple of which referred to Francis Scott Key.

The disk includes a glossary of 179 philatelic terms, but these are only text descriptions. Pictures would be much more suitable for describing many stamp terms, such as line pairs or perfins.

Several articles are provided, such as a beginner's guide to stamp collecting, reference information on Compuserve's electronic stamp club, and addresses for various stamp organizations, periodicals and newspapers.

I have run the first edition of this disk successfully on my Dell computer using both DOS and Windows. I have heard that some Macintosh computer users have encountered problems running the program. Instructions for the second edition do not mention the capability for running the program under DOS.

You can print textual descriptions directly from the CD-ROM when running the program in Windows or on the Macintosh. You can also print stamp images as a full-page picture from the View screen or save the image as a bit-map file, which can later be imported into a graphics program for further manipulation. You should use a BMP extension for your file name as that is the only format that the program will use to store the image. The images are in full color. Figure 22 shows an image of Minkus 40 (George Washington 1860 issue) along with additional information that may be displayed or heard when you press the appropriate button.

Richard Sine took a lot of care in putting the stamp images into the program; they display beautifully on my SVGA moni-

Figure 21.
The main screen of *Encyclopedia of U.S. Postage Stamps*.

tor with 256 colors. You can put the program in a slide-show mode, sit back for about seven hours and look at the individual stamp images as they are displayed with a voice-over description for each one.

The program is worthwhile just for the excellence of its stamp images, but it could use better indexing. The alphabetical index lists Lincoln stamps under A (for Abraham) rather than L for Lincoln, for example. The chronological index, supposedly from earliest to latest, actually lists the 1995 issues first.

Encyclopedia of U.S. Postage Stamps
Richard Sine
100 Poplar Street
Fort Mill, SC 29715
e-mail: Rsine@ix.netcom.com
Price: $32.50 postpaid

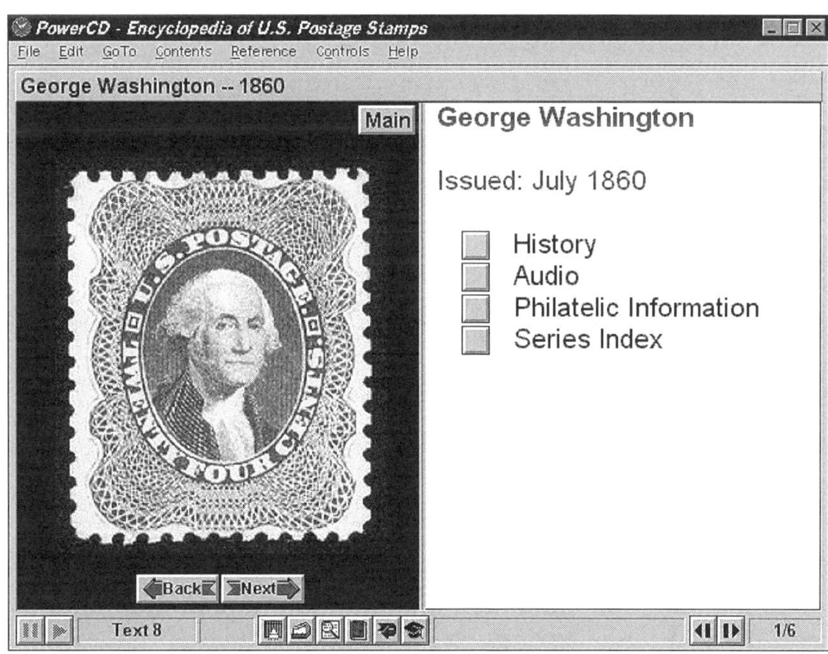

Figure 22.
An image of a 4¢ George Washington stamp of 1860. The image appears in full-color in *Encyclopedia of U.S. Postage Stamps*.

Les Timbres de France et de Monaco

Yvert & Tellier's CD-ROM, *Les Timbres de France & de Monaco*, provides an on-screen catalog of all stamps issued by France and Monaco through 1995. The program also provides two methods of tracking your collection of these stamps: simple and expert.

Installation consists of placing the CD-ROM disk in your CD tray, choosing File Run in Windows and typing x:setup, where x is the drive letter for your CD drive.

According to the Y&T printed documentation, you need at least a multimedia 486 PC with 8 megabytes of memory running Windows 3.1 or later, and a graphics board with 256 colors. Y&T specifies a quad-speed CD-ROM drive, but the program worked fine with my dual-speed drive.

The opening screen, shown in Figure 23, allows you to choose either French or English language display. The main menu, Figure 24, provides a choice of using ei-ther the catalog of France or Monaco, searching for a specific stamp, viewing a video presentation or quitting the program. When you click on either catalog you reach another screen, which allows you to consult, organize or evaluate your collection. The French catalog is divided into four sections, three by dates through 1995, and one for airmail stamps and other issues. Selecting the 1961-95 section brings up a screen that displays the stamps starting with that time period. This display corresponds to the Y&T paper album page, so if you mount your stamps using a Y&T album, it is very simple to coordinate your holdings with the CD-ROM catalog. Figure 25 shows a sample page of 1995 stamps.

Clicking on a stamp image brings up a window that displays an enlarged picture of the stamp along with a description and detailed information about the stamp. Clicking on the magnifying glass on this screen enlarges the stamp to full-screen size. The stamp images are strikingly clear.

You can locate particular stamps us-

Figure 23.
The opening screen of Yvert & Tellier's CD-ROM, *Les Timbres de France et de Monaco.*

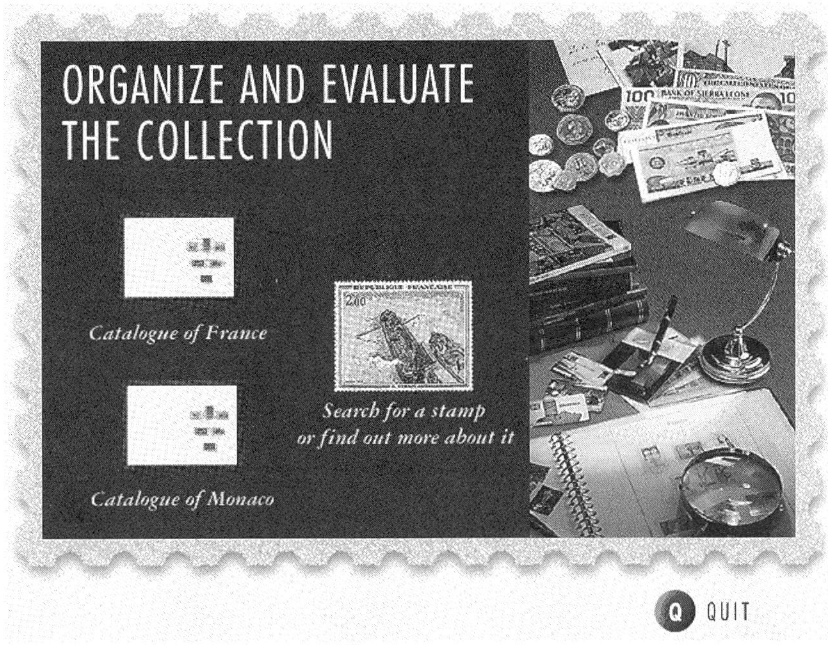

Figure 24.
The main menu of *Les Timbres de France et de Monaco* allows the user to select France or Monaco to search for a stamp.

Figure 25.
A page of 1995 stamps, from the Yvert & Tellier CD-ROM.

ing the search function from the main menu or by clicking on the Research button at the bottom of the screen. You can search by Y&T catalog number, face value, year of issue, theme, subject or even stamp color. It took the program about two seconds to discover that there are 818 red stamps in the French catalog and to display the first group of stamps on the screen.

Two database functions are provided. The simple classification shows on-screen album pages with stamps initially displayed in black and white. For most stamps, you click once on a stamp to indicate that you own a mint unhinged copy. The stamp is then shown in full color. A second click puts a cancel on the stamp; this indicates that you own a used copy. There's an added choice for mint hinged stamps for French catalog numbers between 100 and 1229; these are indicated by an asterisk appearing on the stamp.

The expert classification allows you to specify multiple copies of each stamp and provides an input screen with the Y&T catalog value for each stamp specified. You enter the quantity and a percentage factor, e.g., less than catalog value for a poorer specimen, and the program calculates the total value of your holdings for this stamp.

An evaluation function provides the total value of your collection, but that's the extent of the reporting functions available. As far as I can tell, you'll have to keep track of your collection using French francs. I couldn't find an option to convert to other currencies.

The CD-ROM also includes a glossary function with some text definitions of philatelic terms. It's a short list. Using graphics to illustrate some of these terms would have made this section much more useful.

The graphic stamp images aren't accessible outside the program. They apparently are stored on the CD-ROM in one large 469-megabyte file.

Y&T plans to provide an update CD-ROM annually that will integrate new valuations as well as new stamps issued during the year. The 1996 update is priced at 120FF ($24).

Les Timbres de France et de Monaco
Yvert & Tellier
37, rue des Jacobins
80036 Amiens Cedex 1, France
Phone: (33) 22 71 71 71
Fax: (33) 22 71 71 89
Web address: http://www.Yvert-et-Tellier.fr
    (note the capital letters and the dashes
    between words)
Price: 349 francs (approximately $70)

Ducks '95

Ducks '95 is an unassuming program available on CD-ROM that provides pictures of more than 750 duck stamps.

Generally I object strenuously to programs that don't include documentation, but this program doesn't need any. The inside pages of the CD-ROM cover provide simple installation instructions. Nothing is added to your hard-disk drive other than a program icon in Windows 3.1 Program Manager or a start menu item in Windows 95.

As shown in Figure 26, the program displays a stamp image at the top left of your screen, provides descriptive information on the right and presents a portion of the database of stamps at the bottom of your screen. Clicking your mouse on the stamp image or on the button labeled "Big" will give you a full-screen stamp image. Figure 27 shows a sample full-screen image. You can navigate through the image database by clicking the left and right arrows to move to the previous or next item. If you know the ID number (not quite the Scott number; note that the program uses FD rather than RW for identifying federal duck stamps), you can click on the blank box, type in the ID number and display that stamp image. Just typing in "PA," for example, will bring you to the first stamps issued by Pennsylvania.

You can sort the database by ID number for U.S. issues, for all issues, by artist, subject, year or just foreign issues. Besides the many state issues, the database contains scanned images for Canada, including provinces, Australia, Costa Rica, Iceland, Mexico, New Zealand, Russia, United Kingdom and Venezuela. You can also set up a slide show to display stamps in order or by random image. You can display a catalog listing of values for the stamps.

The CD contains two images for each stamp — one small image for the stamps displayed with the database information and a larger image for the full-screen view.

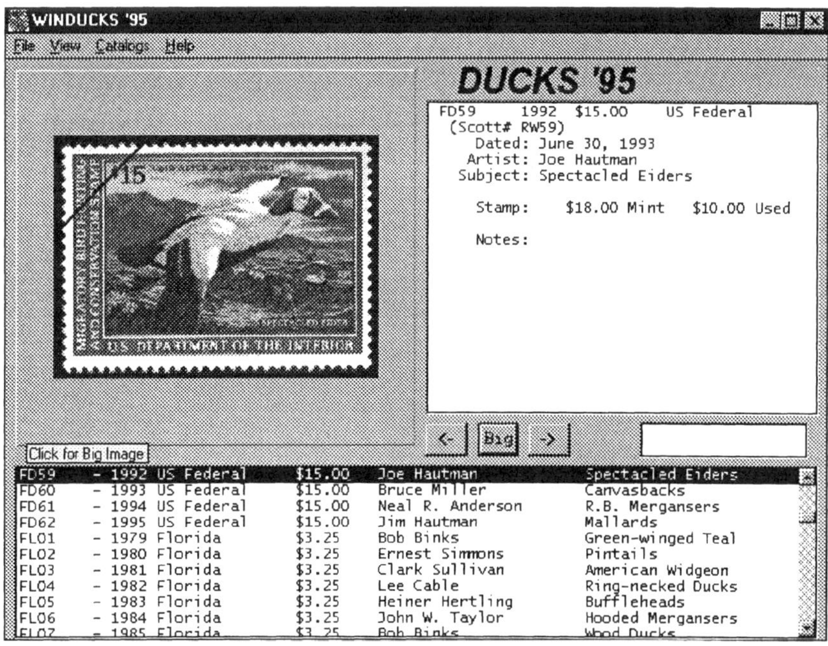

Figure 26.
Ducks '95 displays a stamp image and provides descriptive information as well as the database of stamps.

Figure 27.
A full-screen image from *Ducks '95*.

The small images are each about 43 kilobytes in size; the larger ones, about five times that size. These are standard bitmap images, which can be read by most Windows graphical programs. The images include the standard slanted vertical bar through the left top to avoid copyright and governmental concerns.

The program includes a printing feature that provides a stamp image plus descriptive information about that stamp. Figure 28 is representative. You can also use the screen-capture feature of Windows to copy the program window to the clipboard. You can then paste that window into a suitable graphics program for printing or further manipulation.

One issue that caught my interest was the 1976 Mississippi waterfowl release. The image, shown in Figure 29, is part of an IBM computer punch card. You can see a rectangular hole in the card to the left of and slightly below the number "77." There's some argument as to whether this item can

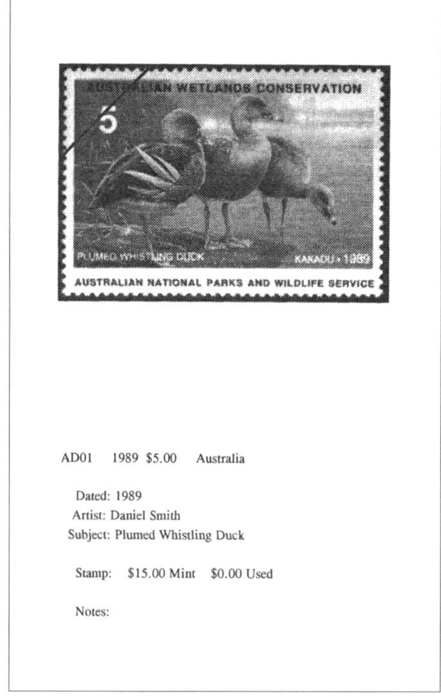

Figure 28.
The printing feature provides a stamp image and descriptive information about the stamp.

really be called a stamp.

You don't need Windows, since there's a DOS version of *Ducks '95* included as a bonus on the CD-ROM. You can't print or use the mouse in this version, but the stamp images appeared cleaner on my screen than in the Windows version. That's somewhat surprising, since the images are provided in a GIF format, which is about half the size of the bitmap format, for the DOS version. You'll need to know which function keys to use to navigate through the program, but a touch of the F1 key provides a listing of what each key does.

The DOS version also provides access to several interesting text files that aren't otherwise available. You'll find background information, including photographs, about Howard Richoux and Dan Harshman, who developed and published the program. Richoux has programmed computers for 25 years; he's been a collector for even longer.

He says that developing the program has given him the most fun he's had in years. He looks forward to seeing additional reference hobby material, not just stamps, becoming available on CD-ROM.

I'm not a duck stamp collector, but I found the text file introducing the subject fascinating. There's a wide range of collecting possibilities, including mint, used, signed (by a hunter, the artist, or perhaps even the governor), on license, as a first-day cover complete with postage. The text file contains color images of items discussed therein.

Ducks '95
Sport'en Art
Ducks CD-ROM Department
1015 West Jackson Street
Sullivan, IL 61951
e-mail: 76350.1772@compuserve.com
Price: $39.95

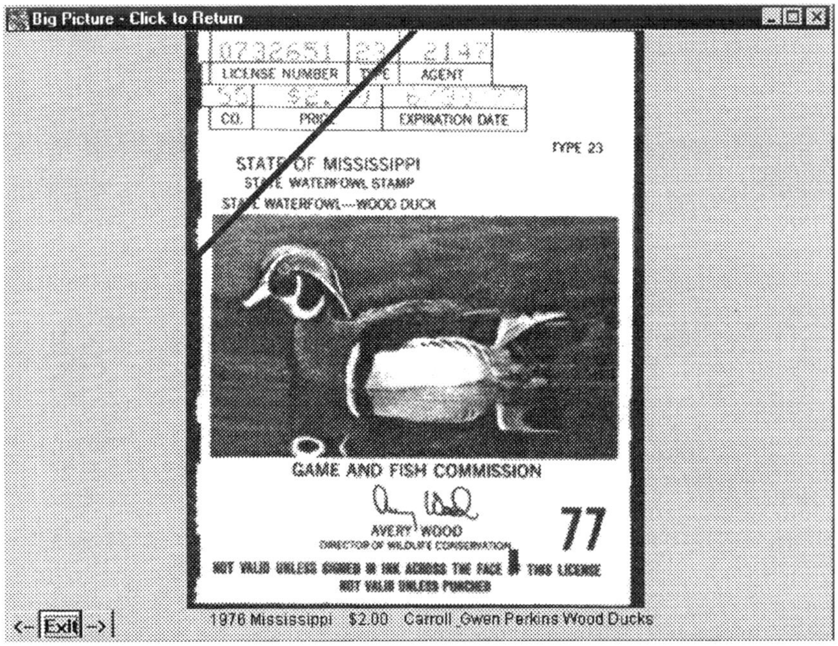

Figure 29.
This 1976 Mississippi Waterfall stamp is part of an IBM computer punch card. The rectangular hole is to the left of and slightly below the number "77."

A Complete Stamp Collection of China

A Complete Stamp Collection of China includes about 10,000 stamps issued by mainland China from 1878 to 1993. The liner notes for the CD state that there are speeches by historical figures, a 30-minute music program and 10 video episodes showing important historical events.

Figure 30 is a screen shot showing a stamp set. If you click the mouse on the magnifying glass on the bottom row of icons, you will see an enlarged image of the first stamp in the set. The text icon provides detailed information (in Chinese) about the stamp. Clicking on the head-phone brings up a sound track that plays one of the musical instruments shown on the stamps.

This disk installs several files on your hard disk and only runs under Windows.

There are a number of ways to search for stamps, including year of issue and Scott number.

A Complete Stamp Collecton of China
China Guide Company
640 Leonard St. 2R
Brooklyn, NY 11222
Phone: (718) 389-4876
Fax: (718) 383-6515
Internet: http://www.china-guide.com
Price: $49

Figure 30.
Users can click the magnifying-glass icon to see an enlarged image of the first stamp in this set.

Stamps of the World

Suggested retail price for *Stamps of the World* is $34.95. You'll need Windows 3.1 and a CD-ROM player. You can obtain additional information by contacting Knowledge Media.

Stamps of the World, A Topical Adventure, provides a gallery of more than 1,800 full-color, computer-enhanced images of stamps from around the world. Fifty countries are represented, arranged primarily in 36 topical groups. There's a search routine included so you can enter a key word to see if any of the stamps match a particular topic.

No catalog numbers or prices are included with this disk, but stamp collectors may nevertheless find some nuggets of information. You'll find details about the American Philatelic Society, selections from Kenmore Stamp's *Finder's Guide to Rare and Valuable Postage Stamps* and several minutes of excerpts from *The Video Guide to Stamp Collecting* hosted by Gary Burghoff.

Michael Pugh, a collector and a Macintosh user, has provided excellent stamp images for the most part. I entered "computer" as a key word for searching, which found two stamps for that topic out of the total 1,800 stamps. Figure 31 shows the screen display for the 1979 Chinese stamp that includes two computers and a set of gears. Topical links for this stamp encompass chemistry and physics, electronics and inventions.

Despite Pugh's Macintosh background, the program is provided in a Microsoft Windows format only. Installation is straightforward: The setup routine copies about 1 megabyte worth of files to your Windows system directory and sets up an icon that appears as a Program Manager group. If your system cannot run animated files, you are prompted to copy additional files from the CD to your hard disk to provide this capability. I tried to run the program using an 800-by-600 screen display but a major portion of the output screen was cut off both vertically and horizontally. I've encountered this problem with other CD-ROMs; switching to the more coarse 640-by-480 display solved the problem.

Installation instructions packed with the CD refer the user to a README file located on the disk. I couldn't find this file, but installation was so simple that the omission didn't seem to matter. There's an 800 number, fax number and mailing address included in case you need to contact the publisher.

The main menu provides eight choices: topical categories, collector's corner, continents, keyword search, topic chooser, reference section, credits and exit.

Choosing topical categories from the main menu will display a list of topics: history, machines, fine arts, animals, natural wonders and science/technology. Subtopics are listed for each of these descriptive items. You'll find 17 stamps related to electronics listed under science/technology, for example.

If you'd rather search by country, you'd select "continents" from the main menu and see the screen shown in Figure 32. You can position the mouse over any of the buttons shown below the map or place it over the desired map area. Clicking the mouse will result in a more detailed map of the area you select. Choosing Oceania, for example, will give you a map of Australia and New Zealand. Click on one of these map areas, and you will be able to look at the stamps from that country that are included in the CD-ROM database.

Selecting "collector's corner" from the main menu brings up a screen with six additional choices that may be of particular interest to collectors or would-be collectors. Some of the detailed screen displays provide text information using very small fonts that are almost unreadable on my 15-inch monitor. The philatelic glossary is adequate but would be greatly improved with the addition of graphics features. A picture of a se-tenant stamp is a big improvement over a description.

My opinion is that this disk is more suited for the novice collector rather than the more experienced one. A companion product, *Chronicles of American Heritage*, featuring U.S. stamps, has been released.

Stamps of the World
Knowledge Media
436 Nunneley Road, Suite B
Paradise, CA 95969
Price: $34.95

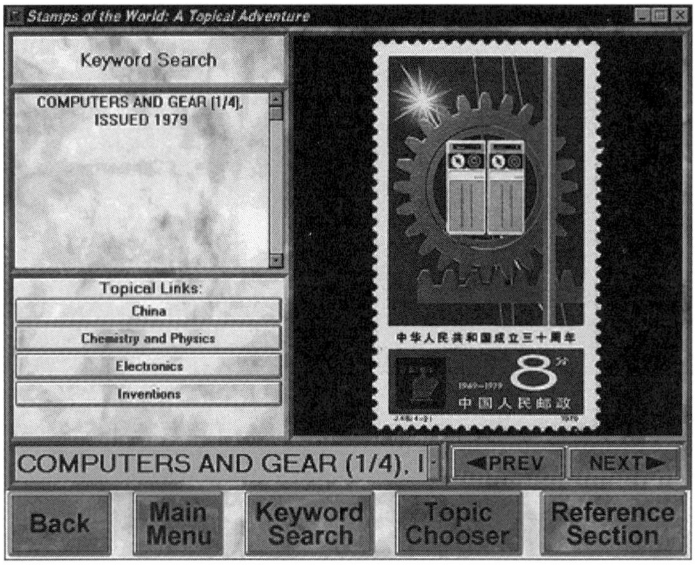

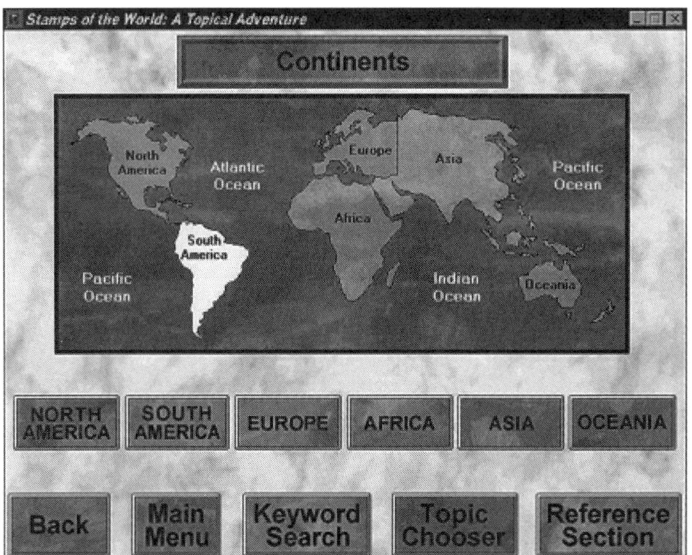

Figure 31.
The screen display for the 1979 stamp showing computers, from the *Stamps of the World* CD-ROM.

Figure 32.
Stamps of the World allows the user to search by country through the continents screen.

Digital Stamp Album

Digital Stamp Album combines a display program and an inventory program. The album program opens as a book (see Figure 33) with background images of the Wizard of Oz and Gone with the Wind stamps on the left and right pages and foreground images of 1995 stamps. Clicking your mouse on an icon on the right side of the volume will open screens about stamp collecting, a reference album, a slide show, a history trivia game and an alphabetical index. Clicking on a stamp image brings up another screen with the stamp image on the left and a brief description on the right. Clicking on this stamp image will display a full-screen image of the stamp.

Stamp images are very sharp; the program uses two scanned images for each stamp — one for the small size and one for the full-screen size.

You move forward and back by clicking on the curled page corners on the left and right top of each page. Double clicking on the magnifying glass at the top of the left page brings up a small dialog box where you can enter any year to display the stamps issued at that time. If you double click on the tongs on the left page, you see a dialogue box for entering the Scott number for any stamp in the database.

The alphabetical index is well-arranged. Note from Figure 34 that you'll find Abraham Lincoln listed under L rather than A. Click on the name in the index and you'll see the image of the first stamp listed. Click on the Scott number of other stamps listed and you'll see the image of that stamp. Retrieval of stamp images was quick, even with my 2x-speed CD-ROM player.

The inventory program, which is installed on your hard disk, is linked with the stamp images on the CD-ROM so you can view an image of your stamp on screen. You'll want to print out the user guide for the inventory program, since there's no manual and no help system, either.

Figure 33.
Digital Stamp Album opens as a book with foreground images
of 1995 stamps.

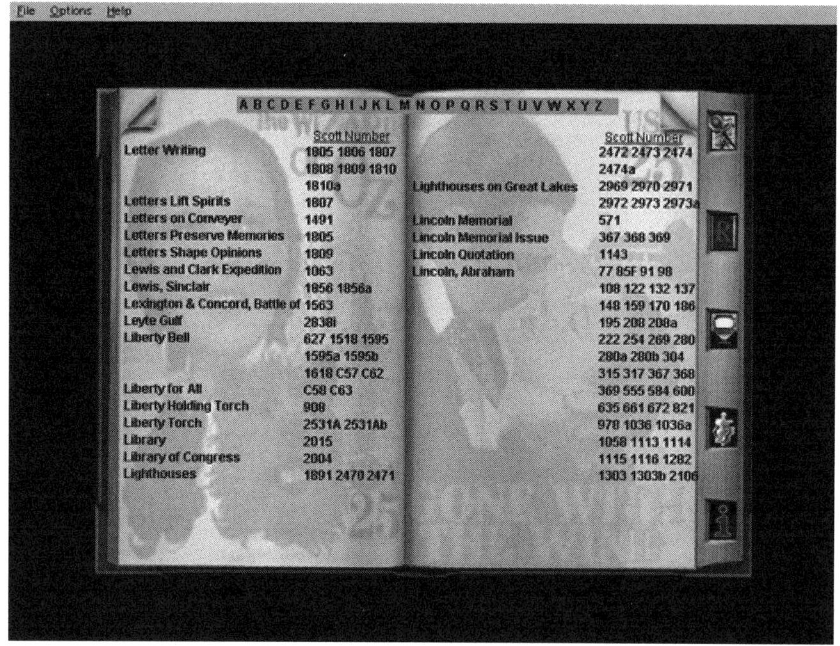

Figure 34.
The alphabetical listing allows the user to click on the name and see the image of the first stamp listed.

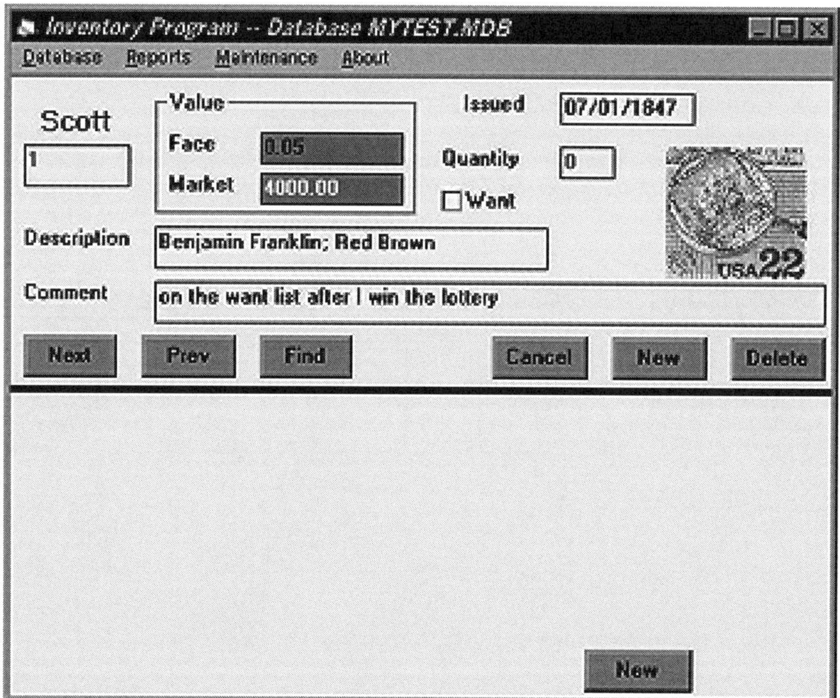

Figure 35.
The inventory program entry form from *Digital Stamp Album*.

The database is handled in two parts: issued stamps, a description of the stamps themselves; and the collection, a description of the stamps in your collection. The first part identifies the stamp by Scott number and includes the face value, date of issue, a text description that you create and the current market value. The second part includes stamp grade, cancellation and gum condition, a purchase date and price, and a field for free-form text comments.

Figure 35 shows the inventory program entry form. The top half of the form covers the first part of the database, which for U.S. stamps is provided by the program. The bottom half provides for entries about the stamps you own. Clicking on the stamp image on the right side of the top part of the form brings up a separate window with an image of that stamp from the CD-ROM. You are not limited to stamps from the CD-ROM, though. You can keep track of foreign collections or add new stamps to your U.S. collection. If you have a stamp image in bitmap format, you can specify the location of your image file and still display it, if desired.

You can create a full or abbreviated report covering your collection, a want list, a sell list and a one-page summary of your collection.

Digital Stamp Album
Walnut Creek CDROM
4041 Pike Lane Suite D
Concord, CA 94520
Phone: (800) 786-9907
Web address: http://www.cdrom.com
Price: $39.95

Multimedia Catalog of Spanish Stamps (1850-1960)

This catalog disk covers Spanish stamps through 1960; it's organized into six distinctive periods, starting with the reign of Isabella II.

You can use the program in either Spanish or English by clicking on the flag emblems shown at the bottom of the opening screen, Figure 36. There are four segments: tutorial, catalog, expert and leisure. The tutorial offers a walk-through of the various screens available. The catalog is the heart of the program, providing access to the stamp images. The expert choice provides information about forgeries. Finally, leisure offers a manipulative puzzle, where the idea is to unscramble an image of a Spanish stamp by moving rectangular blocks around the screen using the mouse (see Figure 37).

In the catalog window, you click on a period to produce an index in chronological order. Click again on a particular series to display stamp images at the bottom of the screen. Click on an individual stamp to see an enlarged digital photo accompanied by text describing its details (see Figure 38). The images are clear; they've been scanned in at 1,200 dots per inch. Clicking anywhere on the image results in an enlargement of that portion of the stamp. The descriptive brochure states that "identifying numbers in the various major stamp catalogs" are displayed, but no catalog numbers showed up in either English or Spanish on my screen.

The expert option provides information on approximately 200 stamps that graphi-

Figure 36.
The opening sceen of the *Multimedia Catalog of Spanish Stamps* allows the user to choose either the Spanish version or English version of the CD-ROM.

cally illustrates the differences between genuine stamps and forgeries. See Figure 39 for an example of this feature. Francesc Graus provided this information. He also appears in a video clip where he discusses forgeries.

No menu option is provided for printing out the images, but you could use a screen-capture program to export the images to another Windows program.

Multimedia Catalog of Spanish Stamps
    (1850-1960)
Afinsa Multimedia
Rambla de Catalunya
91-93-7è 2a 08008 Barcelona, Spain
Phone: (91) 578 04 44
Fax: (91) 575 96 28
Price: 7,500 pesetas (about $60 U.S.)

Figure 37.
This manipulative puzzle offers the opportunity to unscramble an image of a Spanish stamp by moving rectangular blocks around the screen using a mouse.

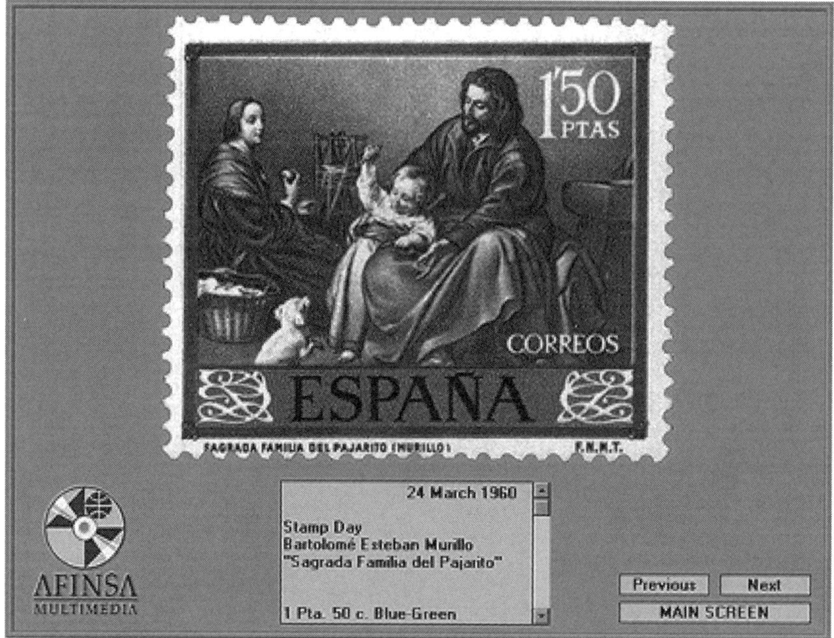

Figure 38.
Enlarged digital photos are accompanied by text describing the stamp's details.

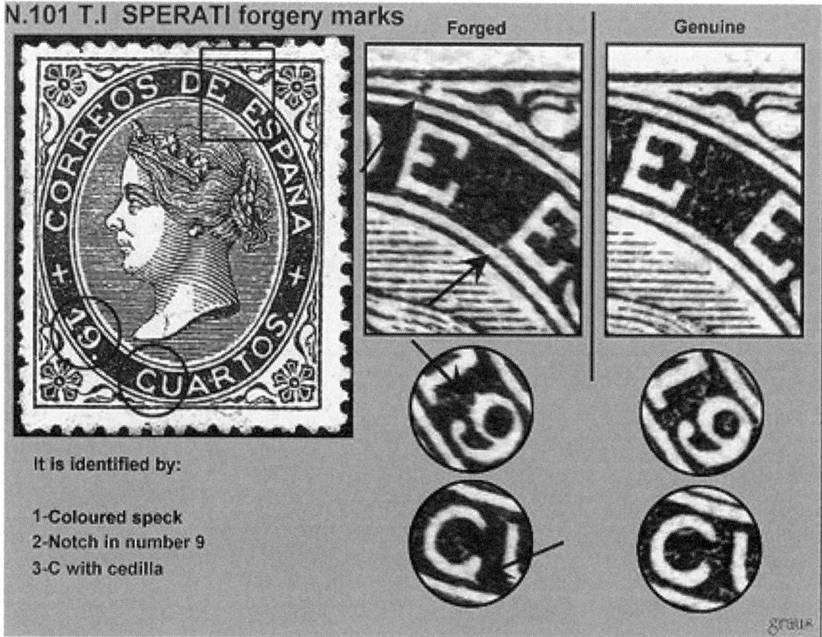

Figure 39.
The differences between genuine stamps and forgeries are shown on screens such as this.

Internet

The Ultimate Information Source for Stamps

What is the Internet? "The Net" is a global network of computers that are connected; actually, it's a loosely organized collection of thousands of networks. It started in the 1970s as the Arpanet, created by the military; it evolved and spread to other organizations, especially universities and libraries. The Internet has become very popular in the last few years mainly because it has become very easy to use and offers a wealth of information on many subjects.

Free Internet access is common in schools, libraries, and other government organizations. You might have free access through your employer. If you want to use your home computer, you'll probably have to pay a monthly charge with extra charges based on usage. Most Internet Service Providers offer unlimited access to the Internet for a monthly fee of $19.95 or less. I have seen advertisements for some local services in the New York and Los Angeles areas where the charges are less than $10 per month for unlimited access. You can also sign up for timed service, usually five hours per month, at a lower rate.

You use the World Wide Web, commonly called "the Web" as a means of searching the Net so that you can move from place to place. Each place on the Web is called a site, and each site has a home page, which is the main page for that site. Each site contains embedded links in the displayed text or graphics; these links lead to other sites with related information. That's the reason the Web can become so addictive; you can move from site to site as you discover information that interests you. And, yes, it's indeed worldwide. A link at one site can lead you to another site in England, France, Australia or other parts of the world.

Links are easily identified within each site. The text of a link is usually a different color than the rest of the text on the page. Links also may be underlined. You simply click your mouse on the link, and you are transported to that site (well, not literally, but your computer screen displays the information from the new site, wherever it may be).

As mentioned in the hardware chapter, you need a modem (the faster the better) for data communications. You also need a starting address for your Web travels. The address is formally known as a URL, or Uniform Resource Locator, which is a long string of letters and symbols. Once you've gotten started, though, you can just click on a link rather than typing additional URLs. Once you've found an interesting site, you can save the site's address as a "bookmark" or "favorite ," making it easy to return to that site in future sessions.

Everything on the Net is subject to change, including URL addresses. I'll be mentioning some addresses in this book that may become outdated. Sometimes that's because the site no longer exists; more often, it's because the address has changed. If you receive a "Site not found" message when you try to reach a location, don't give up. Internet providers include search engines so you can look for sites that contain information you want to reach. Yahoo, Altavista, Webcrawler, Excite and Infoseek all provide search capabilities. You enter one or more words in a dialogue box, then click on a search button, and the search engine returns a list of sites that include those words. If you enter "Stamps" as your text, though, you'll get a very extensive listing that will include a lot of sites unrelated to stamp collecting. You'd be better off entering several words, such as "stamp collecting," "philately" or "United States stamps." The search results include the URL address and a brief description of the site. You can switch directly to the site by clicking on the address. Figure 40 shows the results of an Internet search using Webcrawler.

The most comprehensive site featuring stamp links is Joe Luft's home page, available at:

http://www.execpc.com/~joeluft/.

A June 1997 visit to this site provided a list of 851 links to philatelic-related Internet resources. Luft updates his list regularly; he had added 36 site references in two weeks. Of course, some sites shut down and are deleted from the list. Luft breaks down these links into manageable categories. He includes general philatelic resources, philatelic shows and societies, postal authorities, country-specific resources, sites for down-loading images, collectors' stamp pages, commercial offerings, sources for philatelic software, philatelic autctions and miscellaneous sites. Some of these categories overlap; you can download stamp images from a number of these sources, including images of current and future issues from the U.S. Postal Service.

One of Luft's new additions intrigued me. Since I collect Australian stamps, I couldn't resist clicking on Wombat Lake Stamps, which promised images of Australian issues. I was visitor number 90, based on the odometer reading, which is often shown on web pages to indicate how many users have accessed a site. Figure 41 shows the home page; construction on other pages was still in progress. At the time of my visit, you could view color pictures of 1981 issues only; eventually pictures and descriptions of all Australian stamps will be

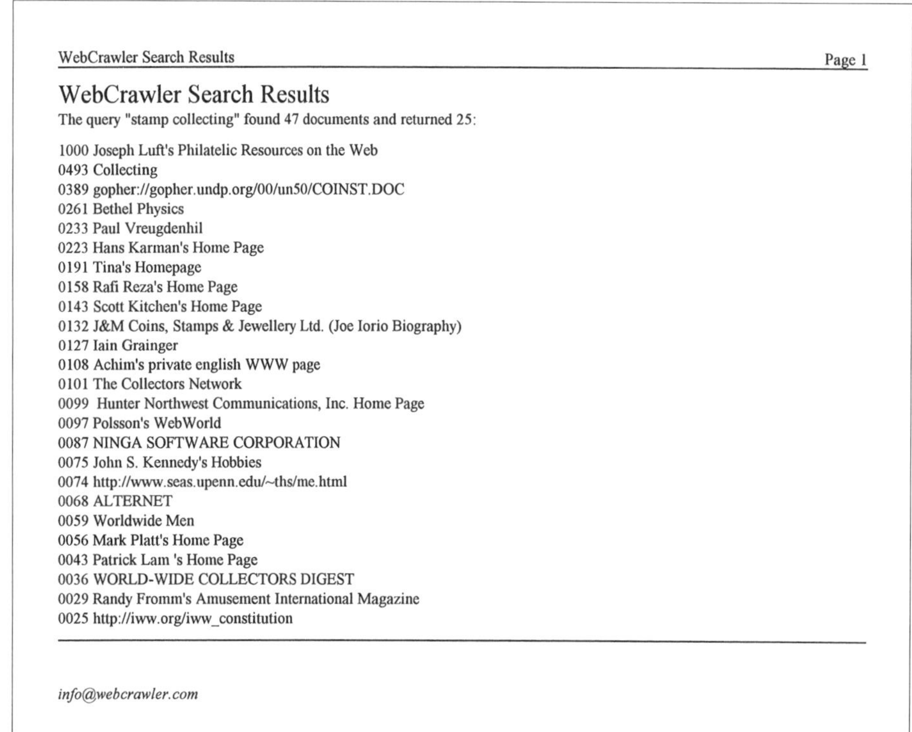

WebCrawler Search Results   Page 1

WebCrawler Search Results

The query "stamp collecting" found 47 documents and returned 25:

1000 Joseph Luft's Philatelic Resources on the Web
0493 Collecting
0389 gopher://gopher.undp.org/00/un50/COINST.DOC
0261 Bethel Physics
0233 Paul Vreugdenhil
0223 Hans Karman's Home Page
0191 Tina's Homepage
0158 Rafi Reza's Home Page
0143 Scott Kitchen's Home Page
0132 J&M Coins, Stamps & Jewellery Ltd. (Joe Iorio Biography)
0127 Iain Grainger
0108 Achim's private english WWW page
0101 The Collectors Network
0099 Hunter Northwest Communications, Inc. Home Page
0097 Polsson's WebWorld
0087 NINGA SOFTWARE CORPORATION
0075 John S. Kennedy's Hobbies
0074 http://www.seas.upenn.edu/~ths/me.html
0068 ALTERNET
0059 Worldwide Men
0056 Mark Platt's Home Page
0043 Patrick Lam 's Home Page
0036 WORLD-WIDE COLLECTORS DIGEST
0029 Randy Fromm's Amusement International Magazine
0025 http://iww.org/iww_constitution

info@webcrawler.com

Figure 40.
The results of an Internet search for "stamp collecting" on WebCrawler.

Figure 41.
The home page of Wombat Lake Stamps.

available. You could also order stamps through this site. The address is http://www.zip.com.au/~womlake/waz/hp2.htm.

A web site, located in Sweden, includes a listing of 600 computer related stamps. The list is sorted alphabetically by country and includes the year issued, the subject, the computer item pictured, denomination, and Scott and Michel catalog numbers. Despite the foreign location, the language used is English. The site also includes a link to V. Gustin's unique web page, which presents a history of computer development as depicted on stamps. There's a chronological text summary with links to individual stamp pictures, which can be downloaded as graphic files or printed as displayed.

The address is www.algonet.se/~heikki/stamp.html

The U.S. Postal Service's site for stamp collectors, StampsOnline, is at: www.stampsonline.com.

This site provides information and excellent pictures of recent and upcoming stamp releases, a general index, stamp news from USPS and a "Just for Kids" area. This last area was "under construction," meaning not quite finished, when I visited the site in October1997 (see Figure 42).

Linn's Stamp News has a web site at www.linns.com (see Figure 43). Here you'll find news stories related to stamp collecting; reference information about stamps; excerpts from the current issue of *Linn's*; selected previous columns; searchable databases of classified ads, stamp shows and auctions; @sk Linn's, a question-and-answer feature; and ordering information for subscriptions, books, and supplies.

Richard Sine has created an Internet magazine for stamp collectors, Net Stamps, located at www.netstamps.com. This is actually a web site with a number of related pages devoted to stamp news. Although the magazine is nominally published once a month, updates are provided as needed throughout the month for breaking news. Each month's issue includes feature articles, including a regular column by Les Winick, departments, and links to other appropriate web sites for collectors. You'll find con-

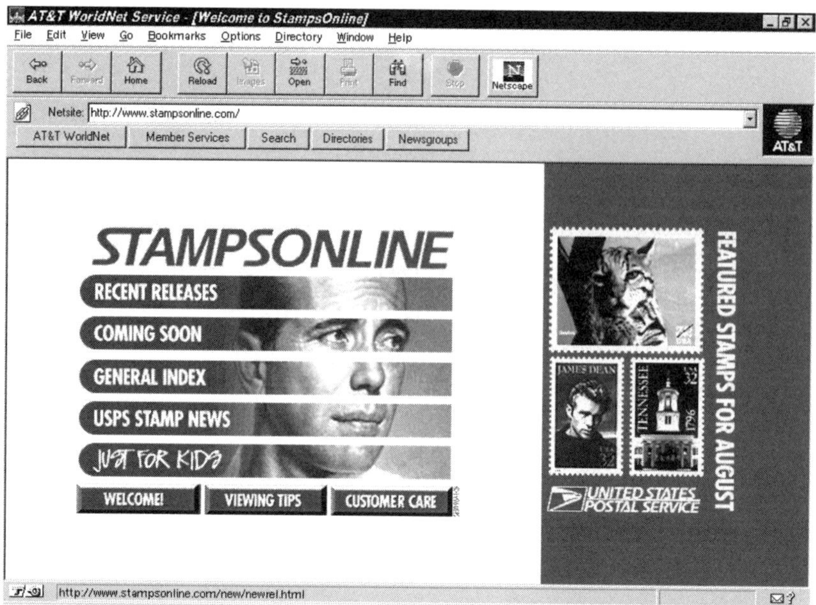

Figure 42.
StampsOnline is the USPS site for stamp collectors.

Figure 43.
The home page of Linn's Stamp News.

troversy here, as well as the opportunity to send e-mail feedback to the editor if you don't like the opinions expressed (see Figure 43).

Usenet is another Internet resource, which offers newsgroups, special areas set up by people who share a common inter-est. Usenet computers store messages sent by users and periodically forward them to other Usenet computers. You can access Usenet to read messages contributed by others and add your own messages. The major categories are quite general, for example "computers," "business," "recre-

Figure 44.
The home page for Net Stamps.

ation." Categories are subdivided by topic, which is further subdivided. The broadest category is Alternative, which has hundreds of topics ranging from therapy to Elvis Presley. You can specify newsgroups in which you are interested and pick up new messages from just these groups.

There's some news in newsgroups, but there's a lot more opinion. A typical group will have experts who dispense wisdom, neophytes who soak it up, and flamers, who like to answer messages with personal insults. You also have lurkers, who read the messages but never post any response.

The newsgroup devoted to stamp collecting, rec.collecting.stamps, is well-behaved, but an occasional argument pops up there, too. Another stamp-related newsgroup is rec.collecting.postal-history. There's also a separate, thorough document titled FAQ for rec.collecting.stamps. FAQ stands for Frequently Asked (or Answered) Questions and is available for many of the newsgroups. FAQ chronicles the most commonly asked questions to keep the newsgroup free of repeatedly asked questions. You'll find an honest representation of rec.collecting.stamps in the following question and answer:

"How does the Usenet philatelic newsletter operate via rec.collecting.stamps?"

"The philatelic news service carried on rec.collecting.stamps is a volunteer approach to promoting the greater exchange of philatelic information through Usenet. The service has no organization, no employees, no legal charter, and no source of income. Rather, it is a bottoms-up approach to communication that exists only to the extent that philatelists contribute articles — particularly those that can be used by newsletter editors.

"The service has no impact on what can be posted on rec.collecting.stamps, where any user can post any message. What the service seeks is an increase in news stories, substantive articles, announcements (e.g., prospectus for an upcoming stamp show exhibition), personal recollections, quizzes, entertainment articles, and so forth. While larger articles are helpful, editors also need filler (short one- or two-paragraph material needed to fill out a column space)."

Chapter 6 of the FAQ covers computer-aided philately specifically. The most frequently mentioned computer uses are making your own album pages, scanning stamp images, and maintaining a stamp database. More web-site addresses are also presented here. There are also detailed questions and answers about inventory, the permanence (or lack thereof) of printer ink and toner, sheet thickness, and the use of scanners. The FAQ is a lengthy document, 27 chapters in all. It provides more than just computer-related information. Chapter 11, for example, covers philatelic terms and abbreviations used in our hobby.

You can also receive mailing lists related to stamps by using the LISTSERV feature of the Internet. You do not need full Internet access to take advantage of this service, but you must be able to receive e-mail.

The on-line services also offer stamp-related forums similar to the newsgroups. These forums have moderators and generally are not as unstructured as newsgroups. The forums also offer libraries where you can download demonstration or sample programs related to stamps. As an example, on the Compuserve online service, typing the keywords "go stamps" will take you to the stamp forum.

Chapter 8

Organizations

Two groups actively provide information and guidance to stamp collectors who may be interested in computers. These groups have different objectives, although each publishes a quarterly journal and each charges $10 in annual dues.

The first group is the Mathematical Study Unit, which publishes *Philamath, a Journal of Mathematical Philately.* Each issue includes articles about mathematics and mathematicians on stamps. The emphasis is on stamps. Larry Dodson has been writing a continuing series (39 articles to date, starting in January 1983) about computers on stamps for *Philamath.* Taken together, these articles are the definitive work on the variety of computer-related subjects that have appeared on stamps and postal stationery.

Dodson has an extensive collection of his own, and he has set up the following categories for computer-related stamps: predecessors, people, data collection, input/output, computer systems, inside the computer, results, combinations, special issues and marginal issues. Dodson includes such items as fingers (used for counting), abacuses, the quipu (a device used for keeping records by tying knots in strings), slide rules, adding machines and calculators as predecessors to the computer. The oldest issue showing fingers used for counting is Mexico Scott C101, issued in 1939.

Illustrations of stamps are generously sprinkled throughout the publication.

The Mathematical Study Unit also provides updates to a checklist of topical items covering mathematical subjects. Computer topicals are a substantial subset of this list with more than 450 stamps in the most recent checklist. The stamps are identified by country, year issued and catalog number. There's no further breakdown on what computer category the stamp fits.

You can obtain information about joining the Mathematical Study Unit by contacting Estelle Buccino, 5615 Glenwood Road, Bethesda, MD 20817. The annual dues of $10 include four issues of the journal. The $10 cost applies to North America. The charge is $15 for other countries.

The Philatelic Computing Study Group is concerned with how a collector may utilize a computer to aid in his enjoyment of his hobby. Here the emphasis is on computers. A typical issue of *The Compulatelist* provides reviews of one or more stamp-inventory and album-page programs, and articles about how collectors use commercial programs as a hobby aid. You'll also find information about computers being used at stamp shows, online addresses for PCSG members, listings and comments about Internet web sites related to stamps, book reviews and announcements of CD-ROMs for collectors.

The journal includes a listing of names and addresses of people who will answer questions about various computers (Apple and IBM-compatibles) and software (dBase, Paradox, spreadsheets, desktop publishing, Microsoft Word and Word Perfect).

You can join PCSG by sending $10 for the first year's dues to PCSG, P.O. Box 5025, Oxnard, CA 93031. For Canada, the dues are $12; for other countries, $15. You can obtain more information about the group by sending a number 10 addressed stamped envelope to the same address. PCSG maintains an Internet presence at http://www.west.net/~stamps1/pcsg.html. Note that the character after the word "stamps" is a "one," not the letter "l."

In addition, the American Topical Association publishes articles about computers on stamps in the bi-monthly publication *Topical Times.* They also maintain a checklist of stamps featuring computers. Contact ATA at P.O. Box 65749, Tucson, AZ 85728.

Glossary

This listing of computer terms is far from comprehensive. It's intended primarily to cover unfamiliar terms that I use elsewhere in this book, as well as some of the more common terms that apply to personal computers. I own a book titled *A Dictionary of Minicomputing and Microcomputing*, by Philip E. Burton. The book was published in 1982 and devotes 344 pages to definitions of computer terms. It's obviously out of date (you won't find WYSIWYG defined in it), but I cite it to indicate the scope of computer terms that were in use about 15 years ago.

application software — computer programs that are designed for specific tasks, such as word processors, spreadsheets, stamp inventory and album-page creation.

backup — a copy of important files. Always back up your data files.

bit — a contraction of "binary digit," which has the value 0 or 1. This is the smallest unit of measurement a digital computer can handle. Think of a bit as a switch. If it's on, the value is 1; if it's off, the value is 0.

byte — usually a group of eight bits that represent one character, such as the letter "a."

CD-ROM (compact disk read-only memory) — similar to music CDs, except these are used to store data. CD-ROMs have been released that store stamp images and related information.

code — instructions that tell a computer what to do.

computer — a device that can accept data (input), store (memory) and execute a program of instructions, perform mathematical, logical and manipulative operations on data (process), and report the results (output).

CPU — central processing unit, the core of the computer. Consists of the logic and circuits where data are processed.

cursor — a movable indicator displayed on screen to assist the user in input. A typical word processor will display a vertical bar (insertion point) indicating where the next character typed will be displayed. See **pointer**.

data — facts or observations about physical phenomena.

database — a collection of logically related records and fields. The Scott catalog would be considered a database. Information about each stamp makes up one record. The catalog number, stamp image, description and prices are fields.

DOS — disk operating system. An operating system is a group of various programs that manages the operation of a computer system. Microsoft DOS has been the main operating system for IBM-compatible machines since 1981 but is now being replaced by Windows 95 and Windows 97. DOS is a text-based operating system.

e-mail — electronic mail; the transmission, storage and distribution of text messages in electronic form over communications networks.

fax — short for facsimile; the transmission of images and their reconstruction at a receiving station.

field — a data element consisting of a grouping of characters that describes a particular attribute, such as the price of a particular stamp.

floppy disk — a small plastic disk coated with iron oxide. It provides a portable form of magnetic media used to store data and programs. "Floppy" refers to the characteristics of the actual thin disk; it's actually protected by a fairly rigid plastic case. The most commonly used PC floppy disk holds 1.44 megabytes of data.

format — the arrangement of data on a medium.

gigabyte (GB) — roughly 1 billion bytes. It's actually 1,073,741,824 bytes, or 2 raised to the 30th power.

hard disk — a magnetic disk device consisting of several metal disks, usually located within the computer case. Typical capacity of hard disks ranges from 100 megabytes to several gigabytes.

hardware — computer equipment you can trip over. It's the computer equipment as opposed to software.

hypertext — a method of indexing text in electronic form so that it can be quickly accessed by a reader.

IBM-compatible — designates a personal computer that runs programs that were designed for IBM machines as opposed to Macintosh computers.

input — raw data that will be entered into a computer. The most common input device is the keyboard.

joystick — a small lever set in a box used to control the screen cursor. It's an alternative to the mouse, commonly used for computer games.

kilobyte (kb or k) — roughly 1,000 bytes. More accurately, it's 1,024 bytes or 2 raised to the 10th power.

media — all tangible objects on which data can be recorded. Includes floppy and hard disks, CD-ROMs and magnetic tape.

megabyte (Mb) — roughly 1 million bytes. The actual number is 1,048,576 or 2 raised to the 20th power. A computer system with 16 megabytes of memory contains 16,777,216 bytes.

megahertz (MHz) — millions of cycles per second. An indicator of how fast a computer operates. Typical PCs operate at speeds from 16 to over 200 MHz.

memory — the place in a computer where information is stored, either temporarily (see **random-access memory**) or permanently (see **read-only memory**).

menu — a displayed list of items from which a user can make a choice, either by clicking a mouse or using keys on the keyboard.

microcomputer — the smallest major category of computers, including personal computers, workstations and network servers. They range in size from portable hand-held units to desktops and floor-standing models.

microprocessor — a single chip containing all the processing circuitry in a computer.

MIPS — millions of instructions per second. An indicator of how fast a computer can operate.

modem — contraction of modulator/demodulator. A device that translates the output of a computer into sounds that can be sent and received over telephone lines.

mouse — a small device that is connected to a computer (the wire is the mouse's tail). You use it by hand on a flat surface to move the pointer on screen in the same direction. Buttons on the mouse (1, 2 or 3) allow users to issue commands or make selections.

multitasking — accomplishing several tasks at the same time on the computer. You could be downloading information from the Internet while working in a word-processing program at the same time.

output — information that has been processed by the computer. The two most common output devices are the screen and the printer.

peripheral — any unit of equipment separate from the central processing unit, that provides the system with input, output or additional storage capabilities. Printers, keyboards and monitors are all peripheral devices.

PC — personal computer. Often refers to an IBM-compatible machine, but a Macintosh computer is also a PC.

pointer — an on-screen indicator positioned by a mouse or other pointing device. It's usually in the shape of an arrow, but may be one of various shapes, depending on what process is being carried out.

program — a series of instructions prepared to achieve a certain result. These instructions are prepared using a variety of programming languages.

random-access memory (RAM) — memory used for temporary storage of data or program instructions. Each memory position can be directly sensed (read) or changed (write) directly. Most PCs contain 8 to 32 megabytes of RAM.

read-only memory (ROM) — memory used for permanent storage. Generally can only be read, not written. PCs contain a small amount of ROM to hold information about the system.

record — a collection of related fields treated as a unit. See **database**.

software — computer programs concerned with the operation of a system. Contrast with **hardware**.

telecommunications — refers to the transmission of signals containing data or images over long distances using phone, radio or satellite technologies.

terabyte — about 1 trillion bytes, actually 2 raised to the 40th power.

trackball — a rollerball set in a case used to move the cursor on screen. Consider it an upside-down mouse. The advantage is that you move the ball rather than the entire mouse, so that you conserve valuable desk space.

user friendly — a term, referring to programs or equipment that are safe, comfortable and easy to use.

virus — code (instructions) that copies an annoying or destructive routine into the computer system.

Windows — with a capital W, this refers to Microsoft Windows. Windows 95 is a graphically oriented (as opposed to text-based DOS) operating system for PCs. Previous versions of Windows through 3.11 are also graphically oriented but are not considered as complete operating systems. With a lowercase w, refers to one portion of a screen that displays information. A Windows screen can have multiple windows, each of which is self-contained. A window can also take up the entire screen.

WYSIWYG — What You See Is What You Get. A description of a graphically oriented program where the information you see on the screen is an almost exact copy of what will be printed on the page, including font size, boldface, italics, underline, margins and diagrams or pictures. Standard in Windows and Macintosh programs; older text-based programs sometimes provide a print-preview mode that approximates this information in a screen view of the printed page.

Linn's Guide to Stamp Collecting Software

Index

About the Author

William F. Sharpe has been writing for *Linn's Stamp News* since 1983. He wrote his first columns using a typewriter, since his Commodore VIC-20 computer didn't include a printer. That early computer didn't have a disk drive or a monitor either. Programs were saved on audio tapes, and a TV set was used as a viewing screen. Sharpe now works with a Dell Pentium computer, a Hewlett-Packard laserjet printer, and an Epson color inkjet printer.

Sharpe retired from aerospace engineering in 1989. A native of Pennsylvania, he graduated from Villanova University with a degree in English and later received a Master's degree in Engineering from the University of Southern California.

He moved to the West Coast three times, finally realizing that this was the spot to settle down in 1970. He and his wife Nancy, who accompanied him in all these cross-country trips, enjoy the relaxed living style in California eight blocks from the beach. They have four children and four grandchildren, all living in California. He teaches computer-science and programming classes part time at the local community college.

His collecting interests include United States and Australian stamps as well as topical stamps such as lighthouses, trolley cars, and computers on stamps. He followed the typical collector pattern, starting his interest in stamps at the high-school level, then putting aside the albums and tongs for about 30 years. An estate sale of stamps rekindled his interest in 1980.

He is a member of the American Philatelic Society, the American Topical Association and the Mathematical Study Unit. He has been the treasurer for the Philatelic Computing Study Group since 1992 and has written articles for that group's newsletter, *The Compulatelist*.